The Intellectual Life

The Intellectual Life

Its Spirit, Conditions, Methods

A.G. Sertillanges, O.P.

translated from the French by Mary Ryan
with a new foreword by James V. Schall, S.J.

The Catholic University of America Press
Washington, D.C.

Nihil Obstat: Jacobus Bastible, S.T.D.
Censor Deputatus

Imprimatur: Daniel
Episcopus Corcagiensis

die 28 Septembris, 1946

This edition published in 1987 by The Catholic University of America Press with the permission of The Mercier Press, Ltd., 4 Bridge St., Cork, Ireland

Reprinted in 1998 with a new foreword

Printed in the United States of America

ISBN 0-8132-0646-4

Contents

Foreword

On the Joys and Travails of Thinking

"A vocation is not fulfilled by vague reading and a few scattered writings."
— A. D. Sertillanges, Preface to the 1934 Edition.

Many of us in later years wish that, when we were younger, someone would have told us about certain things, often certain books that, as we look back on them, would have greatly helped us in the project of our lives, in particular would have helped us know the truth of things. Some of these books are directed to *what is* true, to reality, to what is, but a certain number are rather directed to the question of "how do I go about knowing?" I have in fact written one myself, *Another Sort of Learning* (Ignatius, 1988). In that book, I mention A. D. Sertillanges' book on "the intellectual life" among those few that will give anyone seriously interested a good start.

But Sertillanges gives more than a good start. He explicitly tells how to start, how to read and write, how to discipline our time, indeed our soul. He also attends to the life of the spirit in which any true intellectual life exists. We have perhaps heard from Aristotle that we are rational animals, that the contemplative life is something to which we should aspire. Practically no one tells us what this might mean, whether it is something that is available to us on some condition that we do not easily comprehend. But even if we vaguely know that the intellectual life is an exalted one, we have heard rather less about what acquiring this life might entail. No one spells out its terms and conditions. We are also aware that wisdom comes rather later in life than we might at first have suspected. Yet, we suspect that there were ways that could have helped us had we only known them.

The great French Dominican, A. D. Sertillanges (1863–1948), wrote a book in 1921 which he called *La Vie Intellectuelle*. The book was an immediate success, went through many editions, in many languages. Recently, I recommended this book to a young military officer in graduate school at Indiana University, a man destined to teach at West Point. He told me that he ordered it from The Catholic University of America Press but that, at the time, it was out of print. As I had occasion to write to the Marketing Director at CUA Press, I mentioned that this book needed to be kept in print. And much to her credit, she told me that indeed CUA Press was considering another printing.

Too I remarked that the book probably needed a new introduction. I was worried that computer users, a group that now probably includes most of us, might be put off when they read Sertillanges' advice to take notes on file cards! Even though I recognize that, without my help, any computer user will easily translate Sertillanges' advice into computer practicality, I was concerned lest people think this timeless book was out of date because it was written before the computer was a normal tool. In any case, lo, the good Director at CUA Press wondered if I would like to write one. Indeed I would! In a sense, this brief foreword is simply my statement about why this wonderful, useful book should always be kept in print and why it should always be sought out by young undergraduate and graduate students, by elderly folks, and by everyone in-between. Every time I have used this book in a class, often when I teach a St. Thomas course, I have had undergraduate students tell me later that it was a book they remembered because it taught them much about how to continue their intellectual curiosity in a practical, effective manner not merely in college but throughout their lives.

At first sight, as I intimated, this is a quaint book. At second sight it is an utterly demanding book. Sertillanges painstakingly tells us how to take notes, how to begin to write and to publish, how to organize our notes and behind them our thoughts. Thus, I use the word quaint because we no longer use, as Sertillanges did, pens and early typewriters, but sophisticated computers and printing processes that would have amazed him. But keep in mind that Thomas Aquinas, about whom Sertillanges wrote so well and from whose inspiration this book derives, had perhaps only twenty-five years of productive activity in the thirteenth century. He had none of the mechanisms that even Sertillanges had in the 20s of the XXth century. Yet, Aquinas produced an amount of brilliant and profound matter that is simply astounding.

How did Aquinas ever do it? It is highly doubtful that he would have written more or better if he had the latest computer at his disposal. In fact, in some sense it may have been a hindrance. For St. Thomas developed a great memory and an uncanny capacity to have at his fingertips all the knowledge of the great writers before him, including Scripture. This wisdom took books and reading, of course, even for St. Thomas, but he learned how to do these things. What Sertillanges teaches us is how, in our own way, to imitate the lessons that we can find in the great medieval Dominican about how to lead a proper intellectual life, one suffused with honesty and prayer, with diligent work and, in the end, with the delight of knowing.

In reading Sertillanges' book, we cannot help feeling that he is letting us in on some of the secrets of what went into Aquinas' vast productivity and insight. There are just so many hours in a day, in a week or a month. Sertillanges does not ask us all to give up our daily lives and devote ourselves full time to the intellectual life in the sense that a St. Thomas did. Rather, in his practical way, Sertillanges teaches us how to organize our lives so that we can acquire a solid beginning, hopefully when we are young, and spend the rest of our days building on this solid foundation. In brief, Sertillanges teaches us about habits, about discipline, about, yes, productivity and truth. He thinks that we can lead a true intellectual life if we manage to keep one or two hours a day for serious pursuit of higher things. He is not rigid or impractical here. Moreover, when stated in terms of hours or time, we tend to miss what Sertillanges is driving at.

Any sort of learning, in the beginning, will have drudgery connected with it. We can simply call it a kind of work. We need to come to a point where we begin to delight in what we are knowing, where we cannot wait to get back to our considerations or writings or thoughts on a given topic. Anything *that* is is fascinating. Chesterton, whose own intellectual life seems as vibrant as anyone's in our time, once remarked that there are no such things as uninteresting subjects, only uninterested people. A large part of this "uninterestedness" is precisely because we have never learned how or why to see what is there.

Sertillanges teaches us to examine our lives. He does not neglect to mention that moral faults, both serious ones and light ones, can in fact hinder us from having the freedom from ourselves that enables us to see what is not ourselves, to see *what is*. "Do you want to have an intellectual life?" Sertillanges asks in his own Introduction to his 1934 edition. "Begin by creating within you a zone of silence." We live in a world surrounded by noise, by a kind of unrest that fills our days and nights. We have so many things to distract us, even if sometimes we think they might educate us. Sertillanges is sure we have the time. But he is also sure that we do not notice that we have time because our lives appear to be busy and full. We find the time first by becoming interested, by longing to know. Sertillanges demands an examination of conscience both about our sins and about our use of our time.

An intellectual life, a contemplative life is itself filled with activity, but activity that is purposeful, that wants to know, and to know the truth. What we often call "intellectuals" today are probably not exactly what Sertillanges had in mind when he talked about "the intellectual life." Intellectuals as a class, as Paul Johnson wrote in his book *The Intellectuals,* may well be evolving theories and explanations precisely as a product of their own internal moral disorders. We should never forget that an intellectual life can be a dangerous life. The greatest of vices stem not from the flesh but from the spirit, as Augustine said. The brightest of the angels was the fallen angel. These sober considerations explain the reasons why I like this little book of Sertillanges. He does not hesitate to warn us of the intimate relation between our knowing the truth and our not ordering our own souls to the good. The intellectual life can be and often is a perilous life. But this is no reason to deny its glory. And Sertillanges is very careful to direct us to those things that we pursue because they explain what we are, explain the world and God to us.

When we pick up this book, we will be surprised, no doubt, by its detailed practicality. In one sense, this is a handbook, a step by step direction of what to do first, what next. We are tempted to thinking that the intellectual life is some gigantic insight that comes to us one fine morning while we are shaving or making breakfast. Sertillanges does not deny that some insight can come this way. But the normal course of things will require rather an habitual concern to pursue the truth, to know, to be curious about reality.

This book, moreover, is not primarily for academic professionals, though it will harm not a single one of them. Nor would I call it for everyone—butcher, baker, candlestick maker. But it is for very many and not always just for those who have higher degrees in physics or metaphysics. This is a book that allows us to be free and independent, to know, and to know why we need not be dependent on the media or ideology that often dominate our scene. It is a book that does not exactly "teach" us to know, but it teaches us how to go about knowing and how to continue knowing. The book is designed to keep us inwardly alive precisely by teaching us how to know and grow in knowing, steadily, patiently, yes, critically.

I would put *The Intellectual Life* on the desk of every serious student, and most of the unserious ones. Indeed, Plato said that our very lives are "unserious" in comparison to that of God. Something of that relaxed leisure, of that sense of freedom that comes from knowing and wanting to know is instilled in our souls by this book. Its very possession on our desk or shelves is a constant prod, a visible reminder to us that the intellectual life is not something alien, not something that we have no chance, in our own way, to learn about.

We should read through this classic book, make

its teachings ours after our own manner. Adapting what Sertillanges suggests to our own computer, to our own books, to our own hours of the day or night should be no problem. The book will have an abiding, concrete effect on our lives. If we follow its outlines, it will make us alive in that inner, curious, delightful way that is connoted by the words in this book's magnificent title—The Intellectual Life. I see no reason for settling for anything less. The great French Dominican still teaches us how to learn, but only if we are free enough to let him teach us.

—James V. Schall, S. J.

Georgetown University, Ash Wednesday, 1998

Translator's Note

The book now translated has had an immense circulation in French; and understandably so, for it has much to give to all intellectual workers. Everyone whose business it is to use his mind (or *her* mind, for *his* can be common gender) in any kind of work—philosophy, theology, art, science, literature; education, which touches on all these things; or even only in exercising the inevitable influence of ideas on surroundings—will find rich suggestion in it. Perhaps it will be the central conception that our every effort to reach reality is an approach to the great primal Truth; perhaps the stimulating assurance that the individual vocation is always unique and necessary, for "God does not repeat Himself," or the encouraging doctrine of work "in joy"; perhaps detailed help towards living by these principles.

The Italian witticism *translator, traitor* is a warning. Indeed the translator should be a good craftsman, like the artist-craftsman praised in Ecclesiasticus, who "laboreth night and day . . . and by his continual diligence varieth the figure: he shall give his mind to the resemblance of the picture, and by his watching shall finish the work." Accordingly *quod potui feci*. No pains have been spared to reproduce the author's thought exactly, especially when some turn of the French phrase, the abstract precision of the words, some unexpected comparison, made it necessary to depart from his idiom. The rendering has gained much from the careful criticism and suggestions of Rev. Fr. Anselm Moynihan, O.P., S.T.L., which are hereby gratefully acknowledged.

A very few notes have been added to elucidate some technical words or allusions not immediately obvious to other than French readers.

M.R.

September 25th, 1946.

Preface

The little work now republished has been reprinted many times. It dates from 1920. I had not re-read it, and I wondered whether, looking at the book with a fresh eye and fifteen added years' experience, I should recognize my thought. I find it again, whole and entire, except for shades of difference which I shall not fail to bear in mind in the revision that I am now undertaking. The reason is that in reality these pages have no date. They came from what is deepest in me. I had had them in mind for a quarter of a century when they saw the light of day. I wrote them as one expresses one's essential convictions and pours out one's heart.

What makes me trust that they have struck home is assuredly their wide diffusion; but still more the testimony of innumerable letters: some thanking me for the technical help I gave to intellectual workers; others for the ardor that they said had been aroused in young or older hearts; the greater number for what seemed to the reader a revelation precious above all—that of the spiritual climate proper to the awakening of the thinker, to his evolution, his progress, his inspiration, his work.

That is indeed the principal thing. The mind governs everything; it begins, accomplishes, perseveres, finally achieves. Just as it presides over every increase of knowledge, every creation, it directs the more hidden and more searching effect that the worker produces on himself throughout his career.

I think that I shall not weary the reader if I insist once again on this which is the whole of the vocation of the thinker or speaker, of the writer and the apostle. It really is the preliminary question; it is further the fundamental question and consequently the secret of success.

Do you want to do intellectual work? Begin by creating within you a zone of silence, a habit of recollection, a will to renunciation and detachment which puts you entirely at the disposal of the work; acquire that state of soul unburdened by desire and self-will which is the state of grace of the intellectual worker. Without that you will do nothing, at least nothing worth while.

The intellectual is not self-begotten; he is the son of the Idea, of the Truth, of the creative Word, the Life-giver immanent in His creation. When the thinker thinks rightly, he follows God step by step; he does not follow his own vain fancy. When he gropes and struggles in the effort of research, he is Jacob wrestling with the angel and "strong against God."

Is it not natural, given these conditions, that the man of vocation should put away and deliberately forget his everyday man; that he should throw off everything of him: his frivolity, his irresponsibility, his shrinking from work, his material ambitions, his proud or sensual desires, the instability of his will or the disordered impatience of his longings, his over-readiness to please and his antipathies, his acrimonious moods and his acceptance of current standards, the whole complicated entanglement of impediments which block the road to the True and hinder its victorious conquest?

The fear of God is the beginning of wisdom, says Holy Writ; this filial fear is, at bottom, fear of self. In the intellectual sphere, we might call it attention freed from every inferior preoccupation, and fidelity perpetually alive to the danger of falling away. An intellectual must always be ready to think, that is, to take in a part of the truth conveyed to him by the universe, and prepared for him, at such and such a turning-point, by Providence. The Spirit passes and returns not. Happy the man who holds himself ready not to miss, nay rather to bring about and to utilize, the miraculous encounter!

Every intellectual work begins by a moment of ecstasy; [1] only in the second place does the talent of arrangement, the technique of transitions, connection of ideas, construction, come into play. Now, what is this ecstasy but a flight upwards, away from self, a forgetting to live our own poor life, in order that the object of our delight may live in our thought and in our heart?

Memory itself has a share in this gift. There is an inferior memory, that of the parrot and not of the

[1] Because a man is lifted out of and above himself: Greek *ek-stasis*, out of one's ordinary foothold. (Tr. Note.) See pages 31, 133, 255.

inventor; this memory is an obstruction, closing up the ways of thought in favor of words and fixed formulas. But there is another memory, receptive in every direction, and in a state of perpetual discovery. In its content there is nothing "ready-made"; its gains are seeds of the future; its oracles are promises. Now that kind of memory, too, is ecstatic; it functions in contact with the springs of inspiration; it does not rest complacently in itself; what it contains is still inspiration under the name of remembrance, and the self in which that memory dwells surrenders through it to the inspiring vision of truth quite as much as through research.

What is true of acquisition and pursuit was true of the call at the beginning of our career. After the lingering hesitation of youth, which is so often tormented and perplexed, we had to reach the discovery of ourself, the perception of that secret urge within us, which is directed towards some distant result of which we are not yet clearly conscious. Do you imagine that this is easy? Listening to oneself is a formula that amounts to the same thing as listening to god. It is in the creative Thought that our true being lies, our *self* in its authentic shape. Now this truth of our eternity, which dominates our present and augurs of our future, is revealed to us only in the silence of the soul—that is, in the exclusion of foolish thoughts which lead to a puerile and dissipating indulgence in distraction,[1] in the

[1] *Divertissement.* See note on page 216.

repression of the murmured suggestions that our disordered passions never weary of uttering.

Vocation calls for *response* which, in one effort to surmount self, hears and consents.

It will be the same with the choice of means to success, settling one's way of living, one's society, the organization of one's time, the place to be given to contemplation and to action, to general culture and to one's specialty, to work and to recreation, to necessary concessions and to stern refusals, to the concentration that strengthens the mind and the broader studies that enrich it, to aloofness and to contacts: contacts with men of genius, with one's own group, with nature, or with others in general social life, and so forth. These things also can only be wisely judged of in the moment of ecstasy, when we are close to the eternally true, far from the covetous and passionate self.

And when we have done our part, results and the measure of them will demand the same virtue of acceptance, the same selflessness, the same peace in a Will that is not ours. One achieves what one can, and we need to judge our own capacity so as not on the one hand to underestimate it, or, inversely, not to exceed in the direction of pretentiousness and vain conceit. Whence comes this self-judgment, if not from a steady glance at the impersonally true, and from submission to its verdict, even if it cost us an effort or a secret disappointment?

Great men seem to us men of great boldness; in reality they are more obedient than others. The sovereign voice speaks to them. It is because they are actuated by an instinct which is a prompting of that sovereign voice that they take, always with courage and sometimes with great humility, the place that posterity will later give them—venturing on acts and risking inventions often out of harmony with their time and place and even incurring much sarcasm from their fellows. They are not afraid because, however isolated they may appear to be, they feel that they are not alone. They have on their side the power that finally settles everything. They have a premonition of their empire to come.

We, who have no doubt to conceive a very different kind of humility, must yet draw upon the same lofty source. Height is the measure of littleness. The man who has not the sense of true greatness is easily exultant or easily depressed, sometimes both together. It is because the ant does not consider the giant beetle that he looks down on the tiny gnat; and it is because the walker does not feel the wind from the heights that he lingers on the mountain slopes. Always conscious of the immensity of the true and of the slenderness of our resources, we shall not undertake anything beyond our power, but we shall go on to the limit of our power. We shall rejoice, then, in what has been given us in our measure.

It is not a question of mere measuring. The real point of the remark lies in this, that weak work or pretentious work is always bad work. A life with too ambitious an aim or one content with too low a level is a misdirected life. A tree may have indifferent or magnificent branches and flowers; it does not ask for them and cannot command them; its vegetable soul develops under the action of nature in general and of surrounding influences. Our general nature is the eternal Thought; we draw on it with faculties sprung from it, and with the help that it affords us: there must be a correspondence between what we have received from it in the way of gifts—including courage—and what we may expect of it in the way of results.

How much could be said of this fundamental disposition as it affects a career entirely devoted to the life of thought! I have spoken of the opposition and lack of understanding that the great are exposed to; but these things are the lot also of the little; how can they be resisted without single-minded attachment to the truth, and without complete self-forgetfulness? When the world does not like you it takes its revenge on you; if it happens to like you, it takes its revenge still by corrupting you. Your only resource is to work far from the world, as indifferent to its judgments as you are ready to serve it. It is perhaps best if it rejects you and thus obliges you to fall back on yourself, to grow interiorly, to watch yourself, to deepen yourself. These benefits are in the measure in which we rise above self-interest, that is, in which interest centers on the one thing necessary.

Are we perhaps ourselves exposed to the temptation of disparaging, envying, unjustly criticizing others, of disputing with them? We must then remember that such inclinations, which disturb and cause dissension, injure eternal truth and are incompatible with devotion to it.

In this connection we must remark that at a certain level such disparagement is more apparent than real, and that it has a certain value in forming current opinion. We are often taken in by the way in which the masters speak of one another. They attack one another unmercifully, but they are fully conscious of one another's value, and they attack often unintentionally.

Yet it remains true that general progress needs peace and co-operation, and that it is greatly hindered by pettiness of mind. In face of others' superiority, there is only one honorable attitude: to be glad of it, and then it becomes our own joy, our own good fortune.

A different sort of good fortune may tempt us: that of external success, though, to tell the truth, that is nowadays very rare in the case of a true intellectual. The public as a whole is vulgar and likes only what is vulgar. Edgar Allan Poe's publishers said that they had to pay him less than others because he wrote better than others. I once knew a painter to whom a picture dealer said, "You need some lessons."

"? . . ."

"Yes, to learn not to paint so well."

The man whose heart is set on perfection does not understand that sort of language; he does not consent at any price, or in any form, to cultivate what Baudelaire called the zoocracy. But if his heart began to fail him . . .

Even if we snap our fingers at others' appraisals, are we not exposed within ourselves to the foolish judgments of vanity and instinctive puerility? "Never ignore, never refuse to see what may be thought against your own thought," writes Nietzsche. We are not thinking now of incompetent and superficial critics, but of the homage we ourselves owe to vigilance and integrity. How often one would like to evade a difficulty, to be satisfied with an error, unduly to prefer one's own opinion! Severity with oneself, so favorable to rightness of thought, so helpful in safeguarding it against the thousand dangers of research, is heroism. How can one plead guilty and be glad of one's condemnation, without a boundless love for the truth that gives judgment?

That readiness to admit error is offset, it is true, by an uncompromising adherence to our fundamental persuasions, to those intangible intuitions that are at the bottom of our effort and of our very self-criticism. We cannot build on nothing, and the retouches of the workman do not reach down to the first foundations. What we have won by study and considered carefully must be guarded against unjustified second thoughts and scruples. This is demanded by the love of truth of which we have spoken; it is demanded by the same selflessness, which makes us interest ourselves in what is beyond us and yet has taken up its abode in our consciousness. These evaluations are a delicate matter, but they are necessary. On no account must the supreme certainties be shaken, on which all the work of the intelligence reposes.

We must even be on our guard, again in the name of devotion to truth, against that better which has been so rightly called an enemy of good. It sometimes happens that by widening the field of one's research one impairs it; and it sometimes happens that by investigating beyond some advisable limit, the mind loses its clearness and ends by being merely perplexed. The star that one looks at too intensely and too long, can, by that very fact, give a more and more fitful gleam and end by disappearing from the sky.

The conclusion from all this is not that we must not work in depth, nor that we must neglect that broad culture which is a condition of depth in any domain; but that a sure devotion to the true, without personal passion, without loss of balance, is the corrective of excess.

There is another line of defense against hastiness in our judgments and in the development of our work. One is not dazzled, when one loves the truth, by a brilliant idea set in an aureole of commonplaces. That kind of thing does not yield a real result. The most mediocre mind may hit on an idea, like a rough diamond or a pearl. What is difficult is the cutting of the idea, and, above all, its setting into a jewel of truth which will be the real creation.

"Among the hasty readers of books," says Ramon Fernandez amusingly, "I am inclined to place the author of this book." Yes! But what causes this careless haste which absolves at the outset some less interested and less responsible reader? We shall avoid it by devoting ourselves more earnestly to the true alone.

We shall also avoid plunging into some particular theme that we should like to develop without having first explored its general antecedents and its connection with other subjects. To be long multiple is the condition for being richly one. Unity at the starting point is a mere void. One feels this when one is devoted to high and mysterious truth. Even if one does not use everything that one has learned, the accumulated knowledge gives a hidden resonance to one's words, and this fulness has for its reward the confidence it inspires. It is a great secret to know how to give radiance to an idea by means of its twilight background. It is a further secret to preserve its power of convergence in spite of this radiating quality.

Does failure threaten us or have we already experienced it? This is the time to take refuge in that immutable, unconditional devotion to truth which inspired our effort. "My brain has become my refuge," writes Charles Bonnet. But higher than the brain is the object of its devotion, and that is a very much safer refuge. Even at the cost of suffering, creation is a joy; and, beyond creation, veneration for the idea whence it comes.

Besides, as Foch said, "It is with remainders that battles are won." You have failed in something now, which will prepare you to succeed in something else

—to succeed, in short, as everyone who is worth anything, and who tries, is sure to do.

I want to point out one last effect of the supreme submission to truth of which I have sounded the praise. It puts bounds not only to our personal but to our human pretensions. Reason cannot do everything. Its last step, according to Pascal, is to recognize its limitations. It will only do that if it has submitted to its primal law, which is not its own truth, regarded as its property or its conquest, but the Truth that is impersonal and eternal.

Here there is no limit to honor, by the very fact that presumption is laid aside. Mystery pays. Faith substituted for research carries the mind into vast spheres that it would never of itself have known; and the light of its own domain gains by the fact that distant stars compel it to turn its eyes to the sky. Reason ambitions only a world; faith gives it infinity.

I do not want further to lengthen this discourse. What it contains will necessarily be repeated, since its purpose is to show where the All is to be found.

I have pleaded the claims of that All with an inadequacy of which I am fully conscious and for which I crave pardon. I earnestly wish that my suggestions concerning it, weak as they are, may inspire others to praise it better and to serve it more ardently.

A. G. Sertillanges

December, 1934.

Foreword

Among the works of St. Thomas there is a letter to a certain Brother John, in which are enumerated *Sixteen Precepts for Acquiring the Treasure of Knowledge.*[1] This letter, whether it be authentic or not, must be looked at in itself; it is priceless; we should like to imprint its every word in the inmost being of the Christian thinker. We published it together with the *Prayers* of the same teacher, in which his religious thought is condensed and his soul revealed.[2]

We conceived the idea of commenting on the *Sixteen Precepts,* in order to link up with them things of which it is perhaps useful to remind men of study in our day. In practice, that method seemed rather restrictive; we have chosen to adopt a freer procedure; but the substance of this little volume is none the less entirely Thomistic; it will be found to contain what the master suggests, in the *Sixteen Precepts* and elsewhere, concerning the management of the mind.

1 They are given in Latin and English, with a commentary, in a lecture by Fr. Victor White, O.P., published by Blackfriars, Oxford, December 1944: *St. Thomas Aquinas, De Modo Studendi.*

2 *Les Prieres de Saint Thomas d'Aquin,* traduites et presentees par A.G. Sertillanges. Librairie de l'Art Gatholique, 1920.

This little work has no pretension to replace *Les Sources;* [3] in part it is inspired by that book. The author, doubtless like many another, has not forgotten the stirring he experienced at twenty, when Père Gratry stimulated in him the ardent desire of knowledge.

Let us often remind this age, which so sorely needs light, of the conditions that enable us to get light and to prepare its diffusion by our work.

We shall not speak here of intellectual production in itself; that would be the subject of another volume. But it is one and the same mind that first seeks to enrich itself, and then goes on to expend itself wisely.

Since we shall have to say later that to give out is in this case one of the means of adding to our store, we cannot doubt the identity of the principles which, in the one process as in the other, make our intellectual activity fruitful.

For that reason we may hope to be useful to all.

CHANDOLIN
August 15th, 1920.

[3] Translated into English under the title of *The Well-Springs,* by Stephen J. Brown, S.J., Burns, Oates & Washbourne, 1931.

The Intellectual Life

chapter 1

The Intellectual Vocation

I. *The Intellectual Has a Sacred Call*
II. *The Intellectual Does Not Stand Alone*
III. *The Intellectual Belongs to His Time*

I

When we speak of vocation, we refer to those who intend to make intellectual work their life, whether they are entirely free to give themselves up to study, or whether, though engaged in some calling, they hold happily in reserve, as a supplement of their activity and as a reward, the development and deepening of their mind.

I say the deepening, in order to set aside the idea of a superficial tincture of knowledge. A vocation is not fulfilled by vague reading and a few scattered writings. It requires penetration and continuity and methodical effort, so as to attain a fulness of development which will correspond to the call of the Spirit, and to the resources that it has pleased Him to bestow on us.

This call is not to be taken for granted. To start precipitately on a road which one could not tread with a firm step would be merely to prepare the way for disillusionment. Everyone has the duty to work; and after a first early and toilsome training no one acts wisely if he lets his mind fall gradually back into its primitive ignorance; but the effortless maintenance of what one has acquired is one thing, and it is quite another to consolidate from the foundations upwards a sum of knowledge recognized as merely provisional, seen to be simply and solely a starting-point.

This second state of mind is that of one who has the vocation. It implies a serious resolution. The life of study is austere and imposes grave obligations. It pays, it pays richly; but it exacts an initial outlay that few are capable of. The athletes of the mind, like those of the playing field, must be prepared for privations, long training, a sometimes superhuman tenacity. We must give ourselves from the heart, if truth is to give itself to us. Truth serves only its slaves.

This way of life must not be entered on without long self-examination. The intellectual vocation is like every other: it is written in our instincts, in our powers, in a sort of inner impulse of which reason must judge. Our dispositions are like the chemical properties which determine, for every body, the combinations into which that body can enter. A vocation is something that cannot be had for the asking. It comes from heaven and from our first nature. The whole point is to be docile to God and to oneself as soon as they have spoken.

Understood in this sense, Disraeli's saying that you may do what you please, provided it really pleases you, contains a great meaning. Our liking, if correlated to our fundamental tendencies and to our aptitudes, is an excellent judge. If St. Thomas could say that pleasure characterizes functions and may serve to classify men, he must be led to conclude that pleasure can also reveal our vocation. Only we must search down into the depths where liking and the spontaneous impulse are linked up with the gifts of God and His providence.

Besides the immense interest of realizing oneself in one's fulness, the investigation into an intellectual vocation has a more general interest which no one may disregard.

Christianized humanity is made up of various personalities, no one of which can refuse to function without impoverishing the group and without depriving the eternal Christ of a part of His kingdom. Christ reigns by unfolding Himself in men. Every life of one of His members is a characteristic moment of His duration; every individual man and Christian is an instance, incommunicable, unique, and therefore necessary, of the extension of the "spiritual body." If you are designated as a light bearer, do not go and hide under the bushel the gleam or the flame expected from you in the house of the Father of all. Love truth and its fruits of life, for yourself and for others; devote to study and to the profitable use of study the best part of your time and your heart.

All roads but one are bad roads for you, since they diverge from the direction in which your action is expected and required. Do not prove faithless to God, to your brethren and to yourself by rejecting a sacred call.

That presupposes you to come to the intellectual life with unselfish motives, not through ambition or foolish vanity. The jingling bells of publicity tempt only frivolous minds. Ambition offends eternal truth by subordinating truth to itself. Is it not a sacrilege to play with the questions that dominate life and death, with mysterious nature, with God—to achieve some literary or philosophical celebrity at the expense of the true and independently of the true? Such aims, and especially the first mentioned, would not sustain the seeker; his effort would speedily be seen to slacken, his vanity to fall back on some empty satisfaction, with no care for the reality of things.

But it presupposes also that to the acceptance of the end you add the acceptance of the means; otherwise there would be no real obedience to your vocation. Many people would like to possess knowledge! A vague aspiration turns the eyes of the multitude towards horizons that the greater number admire from afar off, as the victim of gout or asthma looks up to the eternal snows. To get something without paying for it is the universal desire; but it is the desire of cowardly hearts and weak brains. The universe does not respond to the first murmured request, and the light of God does not shine under your study lamp unless your soul asks for it with persistent effort.

You are consecrated by your vocation. Will what truth wills; consent for the sake of truth to bestir yourself, to take up your abode within its proper realm, to organize your life, and, realizing your inexperience, to learn from the experience of others.

"If youth but knew!" The young, above all, need this warning. Science in the broad meaning of the word, *scientia,* is knowledge through causes; but actively, as to its attainment, it is a creation by causes. We must recognize and adopt the causes of knowledge, then provide them, and not defer attention to the foundations of our building until the moment of putting up the roof.

In the first free years after early studies, when the ground of our intelligence has been newly turned-up, and the seed sown, what splendid tillage could be undertaken! That is the time that will never come again, the time that we shall have to live on by and by. What it is, we shall be; for we can hardly put down new roots. The future is always the heir of the past; the penalty for neglecting, at the right time, to prepare it, is to live on the surface of things. Let each one think of that, while thinking may be of some avail.

How many young people, with the pretension to become workers, miserably waste their days, their strength, the vigor of their intelligence, their ideal! Either they do not work—there is time enough!—or they work badly, capriciously, without knowing what they are nor where they want to go nor how to get there. Lectures, reading, choice of companions, the proper proportion of work and rest, of solitude and activity, of general culture and specialization, the spirit of study, the art of picking out and utilizing data gained, some provisional output which will give an idea of what the future work is to be, the virtues to be acquired and developed, —nothing of all that is thought out and no satisfactory fulfillment will follow.

What a difference, supposing equal resources, between the man who understands and looks ahead, and the man who proceeds at haphazard! "Genius is long patience," but it must be organized and intelligent patience. One does not need extraordinary gifts to carry some work through; average superiority suffices; the rest depends on energy and wise application of energy. It is as with a conscientious workman, careful and steady at his task: he gets somewhere, while an inventive genius is often merely an embittered failure.

What I have just said is true of everyone. But I apply it especially to those who know that they have at their disposal only a part of their life, the least part, in which to give themselves to the labors of the mind. They, more than others, must be men consecrated by their vocation. What they cannot spread out over all their years, they must concentrate in a small space. The special asceticism and the heroic virtue of the intellectual worker must be their daily portion. But if they consent to this double self-offering, I tell them in the name of the God of truth not to lose courage.

If genius is not necessary for production, still less is it necessary to have entire liberty. What is more, liberty presents pitfalls that rigorous obligations may help us to avoid. A stream narrowly hemmed-in by its banks will flow more impetuously. The discipline of some occupation is an excellent school; it bears fruit in the hours of studious leisure. The very constraint will make you concentrate better, you will learn the value of time, you will take eager refuge in those rare hours during which, the claims of duty satisfied, you can turn to your ideal and enjoy the relaxation of some chosen activity after the labor imposed by the hard necessity of getting a livelihood.

The worker who thus finds in a fresh effort the reward of previous effort, who prizes it as a miser prizes his hoard, is usually passionately devoted to his ideal; he cannot be turned aside from a purpose thus consecrated by sacrifice. If his progress seems slower, he is capable of getting farther. Like the poor drudging tortoise, he does not dawdle, he persists, and in a few years' time he will have outstripped the indolent hare whose agile movements were the envy of his own lumbering gait.

The same is true of the isolated worker, deprived of intellectual resources and stimulating society, buried in some little provincial spot, where he seems condemned to stagnate, exiled far from rich libraries, brilliant lectures, an eagerly responsive public, possessing only himself and obliged to draw solely on that inalienable capital.

He must not lose courage either. Though he have everything against him, let him but keep possession of himself and be content with that. An ardent heart has more chance of achieving something than a crammed head abusing the opportunities of great cities. Here again strength may spring from difficulty. It is in the steep mountain passes that one bends and strains; level paths allow one to relax, and a state of uncontrolled relaxation quickly becomes fatal.

The most valuable thing of all is will, a deeply-rooted will; to will to be somebody, to achieve something; to be even now in desire that somebody, recognizable by his ideal. Everything else always settles itself. There are books everywhere and only a few are necessary. Society, stimulation, one finds these in spirit in one's solitude: the great are there, present to those who call on them, and the great ages behind impel the ardent thinker forward. As to lectures, those who can have them do not follow them or follow them but ill, if they have not in themselves, at need, the wherewithal to do without such fortunate help. As to the public, if it sometimes stimulates, it often disturbs, scatters the mind; and by going to pick up two pennies in the street, you may lose a fortune. An impassioned solitude is better, for there every seed produces a hundredfold, and every ray of sunlight suffuses the whole landscape with autumnal gold.

St. Thomas of Aquin, as he was coming to settle in Paris and descried the great city in the distance, said to the brother who was with him: "Brother, I would give all that for the commentary of Chrysostom on St. Matthew." When one feels like that, it does not matter where one is nor what resources one has, one is stamped with the seal; one is of the elect of the Spirit; one has only to persevere, and to trust life, as it is ruled for us by God.

You, young man who understand this language and to whom the heroes of the mind seem mysteriously to beckon, but who fear to lack the necessary means, listen to me. Have you two hours a day? Can you undertake to keep them jealously, to use them ardently, and then, being of those who have authority in the Kingdom of God, can you drink the chalice of which these pages would wish to make you savor the exquisite and bitter taste? If so, have confidence. Nay, rest in quiet certainty.

If you are compelled to earn your living, at least you will earn it without sacrificing, as so many do, the liberty of your soul. If you are alone, you will but be more violently thrown back on your noble purposes. Most great men followed some calling. Many have declared that the two hours I postulate suffice for an intellectual career. Learn to make the best use of that limited time; plunge every day of your life into the spring which quenches and yet ever renews your thirst.

Do you want to have a humble share in perpetuating wisdom among men, in gathering up the inheritance of the ages, in formulating the rules of the mind for the present time, in discovering facts and causes, in turning men's wandering eyes towards first causes and their hearts towards supreme ends, in reviving if necessary some dying flame, in organizing the propaganda of truth and goodness? That is the lot reserved for you. It is surely worth a little extra sacrifice; it is worth steadily pursuing with jealous passion.

The study and practice of what Père Gratry calls Living Logic, that is, the development of our mind, the human word, by contact direct or indirect with the Spirit and the Divine Word—that serious study and persevering practice will give you entry into the wondrous sanctuary. You will be of those who grow, who enrich themselves, and who make ready to receive magnificent gifts. You too, one day, if God so wills, will have a place in the assembly of noble minds.

II

It is another characteristic of the intellectual vocation that the Christian worker who is consecrated by his call must not be an isolated unit. Whatever be his position, however alone or hidden we suppose him to be materially, he must not yield to the lure of individualism, which is a distorted image of Christian personality.

As life-giving as is solitude, so paralyzing and sterilizing is isolation.

By being only a soul, one ceases to be a man, Victor Hugo would say. Isolation is inhuman; for to work in human fashion is to work with the feeling for man, his needs, his greatness, and the solidarity which binds us closely together in a common life.

A Christian worker should live constantly in the universal, in history. Since he lives with Jesus Christ he cannot separate times, nor men, from

Him. Real life is a life in common, an immense family life with charity for its law; if study is to be an act of life, not an art pursued for art's sake and an appropriation of mere abstractions, it must submit to be governed by this law of oneness of heart. "We pray before the crucifix," says Gratry—we must also work before the crucifix—"but the true cross is not isolated from the earth."

A true Christian will have ever before his eyes the image of this globe, on which the Cross is planted, on which needy men wander and suffer, all over which the redeeming Blood, in numberless streams, flows to meet them. The light that he has confers on him a priesthood; the light that he seeks to acquire supposes an implicit promise that he will share it. Every truth is practical; the most apparently abstract, the loftiest, is also the most practical. Every truth is life, direction, a way leading to the end of man. And therefore Jesus Christ made this unique assertion: "I am the Way, the Truth, and the Life."

Work always then with the idea of some utilization, as the Gospel speaks. Listen to the murmur of the human race all about you; pick out certain individuals of certain groups whose need you know, find out what may bring them out of their night and ennoble them; what in any measure may save them. The only holy truths are redeeming truths; and was it not in view of our work as of everything else that the Apostle said: "This is the will of God, your sanctification?"

Jesus Christ needs our minds for His work, as on

earth He needed His own human mind. He has gone, but we continue Him; we have that measureless honor. We are His members, therefore have a share in His spirit, are therefore His cooperators. He acts outwardly through us, and inwardly through the inspirations of His Spirit, as in His lifetime He acted outwardly by His voice, inwardly by His grace. Our work being a necessary part of that action, let us work as Jesus meditated—as He drew on the life-springs of the Father to pour them out on the world.

III

And then reflect that if all times are equal before God, if His eternity is a radiant center from which all points on the circumference of time are at an equal distance, it is not the same with the ages and with us, who dwell on the circumference. We are here at a given point on the mighty wheel, not elsewhere. If we are here, it is because God has placed us here. Every moment of duration concerns us, and every age is our neighbor, as well as every man; but the word "neighbor" is a relative word to which the wisdom of Providence attaches a precise meaning for each of us, and to which each of us, in submissive wisdom, must also attach a precise meaning.

Here I am, a man of the 20th century, living in a time of permanent drama, witnessing upheavals such as perhaps the globe never before saw since the mountains rose and the seas were driven into their caverns. What have I to do for this panting, palpitating century? More than ever before thought is waiting for men, and men for thought. The world is in danger for lack of life-giving maxims. We are in a train rushing ahead at top speed, no signals visible. The planet is going it knows not where, its law has failed it: who will give it back its sun?

All this is not intended to narrow down the field of intellectual research and to confine it to exclusively religious study. That will be evident. I have already said that every truth is practical, that every truth has a saving power. But I am indicating a spirit, and this spirit, both in general and because of what is opportune at the present time excludes mere dilettantism.

It also excludes a certain archaeological tendency, a love of the past which turns away from present suffering, an esteem for the past which seems not to recognize the universal presence of God. Every age is not as good as every other, but all ages are Christian ages, and there is one which for us, and in practice, surpasses them all: our own. In view of it are our inborn resources, our graces of today and tomorrow, and consequently the efforts that we must make in order to correspond with them.

Let us not be like those people who always seem to be pallbearers at the funeral of the past. Let us utilize, by living, the qualities of the dead. Truth is ever new. Like the grass of morning, moist with glistening dew, all the old virtues are waiting to spring up afresh. God does not grow old. We must help our God to renew, not the buried past and the chronicles of a vanished world, but the eternal face of the earth.

Such is the spirit of the Catholic intellectual, such is his vocation. The sooner he gives precision to this general idea by finding out what kind of study is right for him, the better.

Listen now to the virtues that God asks of him.

chapter 2

The Virtues of a Catholic Intellectual

I

I might say that virtue potentially contains intellectuality, for, since it leads to our end, which is intellectual, virtue is equivalent to the supreme knowledge.

One could draw many things from that, everything indeed; for this primacy of the moral order involves the relative dependence of truth, of beauty, of harmony, of unity, of being itself with regard to morality, which is thus related to the first principle of all things.

But I prefer to follow a humbler path.

The qualities of character have a preponderant role in everything. The intellect is only a tool; the handling of it determines the nature of its effects. Properly to regulate the intelligence, is it not evident that qualities quite different from intelligence itself are required? Instinctively, every right mind declares that superiority in any branch includes a measure of spiritual superiority. To judge truly, you must be great.

Would there not be something repellent in seeing a great discovery made by an unprincipled rascal? The unspoiled instinct of a simple man would be grievously hurt by it. There is something shocking in a dissociation which dislocates the harmony of the human being. One has no faith in jewel merchants who sell pearls and wear none. To be in close contact with the great spring of all things without acquiring anything of its moral nature seems a paradox. To enjoy the faculty of intelligence, and to make of it an isolated force, a "bump," is, one suspects, a dangerous game; for every isolated force in a balanced whole becomes the victim of its surroundings.

If then character makes shipwreck, one must expect the sense of the great truths to suffer. The mind, being no longer held in check, no longer finding its level, will start down some dangerous incline, and one knows that a small error in the beginning becomes great in the end. The force of logic may send to a more precipitous fall the man whose faculty of discernment finds no safeguard in his soul. That is the cause of so many sensational lapses, and of so many blunders with a spark of genius in them, among masters who have lost the true direction of life.

Life is a unity: it would be very surprising if we could give fullest play to one of its functions while neglecting the other, or if to live our ideas should not help us to perceive them.

What is the source of this unity of life? Love. "Tell me what you love, I will tell you what you are." Love is the beginning of everything in us; and that starting point which is common to knowledge and practice cannot fail to make the right paths of both in a certain measure interdependent.

Truth visits those who love her, who surrender to her, and this love cannot be without virtue. For this reason, in spite of his possible defects, the man of genius at work is already virtuous; it would suffice for his holiness if he were more completely his true self.

The true springs up in the same soil as the good: their roots communicate. Broken from the common root and therefore less in contact with the soil, one or other suffers; the soul grows anemic or the mind wilts. On the contrary, by feeding the mind on truth one enlightens the conscience, by fostering good one guides knowledge.

By practising the truth that we know, we merit the truth that we do not yet know. We merit it in the sight of God; we merit it also with a merit which brings its own reward; for all truths are linked together, and homage in act being the most decisive of all, when we pay that homage by living the truth of life, we draw near to the supreme light and to all that flows from it.[1] If I embark on the tributary, I reach the river, and then the sea.

[1] The virtue called truth, says St. Thomas, "is a certain truth according to which a man in word and deed shows

Let us look a little more closely into this doctrine which is so important,—so important that simply to recall it would have made the writing of this little work worthwhile.

Is not virtue the health of the soul? And who will say that health does not affect the sight? Ask the oculist. An intelligent practitioner is not satisfied with measuring the curve of the crystalline lens and choosing glasses, he does not merely advise ointments and lotions; he is curious about your general health, your teeth, your regime, your internal organs. Do not be surprised if that specialist in a single organ even questions you about your moral conduct.

The sight of the spirit is no less exacting.

Do you believe that we think with the intelligence only? Are we merely a bundle of faculties among which for this or for that purpose we select the desired instrument? We think "with our whole soul," declared Plato. Presently we shall go much farther, we shall say: with our whole being. Knowledge involves everything in us, from the vital principle to the chemical composition of the least cell. Mental disorders of every sort, states of delirium, hallucinations, asthenia and hypersthenia, inadaptation to reality of whatever kind, prove that it is not the mind alone that thinks, but the man.

---

himself as he is." The truth of life "is particularly so called according as a man in his life fulfils what he is ordained to by the divine intelligence." S.T.Ia, qu. 16, art. 4, ad 3. (Tr. Note.)

How will you manage to think rightly with a sick soul, a heart ravaged by vice, pulled this way and that by passion, dragged astray by violent or guilty love? There is, Gratry said, a clear-sighted and a blind state of the soul; a sound and therefore sensible state, and a state of folly. "The exercise of the moral virtues," St. Thomas of Aquin tells you in his turn, "of the virtues by which the passions are held in check, is of great importance for the acquisition of knowledge." [1]

Yes indeed! Think it out. On what, first and foremost, does all the effort of study depend? On attention, which delimits the field for research, concentrates on it, brings all our powers to bear on it; next, on judgment, which gathers up the fruit of investigation. Now, passions and vices relax attention, scatter it, lead it astray; and they injure the judgment in roundabout ways, of which Aristotle and many others after him have scrutinized the meanders.

All contemporary psychologists are in agreement here; the fact is plain to see, admitting of no doubt. The "psychology of the feelings" governs practice, but also, to a large extent, thought. Knowledge depends on the direction given to our passions and on our moral habits. To calm our passions is to awaken in ourselves the sense of the universal; to correct ourselves is to bring out the sense of the true.

Carry your analysis further. What are the enemies of knowledge? Plainly, lack of intelligence; there-

[1] VII Physic., lib. 6.

fore in discussing vices and virtues and their role in the pursuit of knowledge we presuppose persons who are equal in other respects. But, stupidity apart, what enemies do you fear? What about sloth, the grave of the best gifts? What of sensuality, which makes the body weak and lethargic, befogs the imagination, dulls the intelligence, scatters the memory? Of pride, which sometimes dazzles and sometimes darkens, which so drives us in the direction of our own opinion that the universal sense may escape us? Of envy, which obstinately refuses to acknowledge some light other than our own? Of irritation which repels criticism and comes to grief on the rock of error?

Without these obstacles, a man of study will rise to heights greater or less according to his resources and his environment; but he will reach the level of his own gifts, of his own destiny.

We must notice that all the faults just mentioned bring one another more or less in their train; they intersect, they ramify, they are with regard to love of the good or contempt for the good what intersecting streamlets are to the spring. Purity of thought requires purity of soul; that is a general and undeniable truth. The neophyte of knowledge should let it sink deeply into his mind.

Let us rise higher, and speaking of springs, let us not forget the Supreme Spring. The surest metaphysic tells us that at the summit of things, the true and the good are not only connected, but are identical.

We must state for exactness' sake, that the good

thus spoken of is not properly speaking *moral* good; *desirable* good is what is directly referred to; but a little circuit brings us back from the latter to the former.

Moral good is nothing else than desirable good measured by reason and set before the will as an end. Ends are related. They all depend on one ultimate end. It is this ultimate end which links up with the true and is one with it. Connect these propositions, and you will find that moral good, if not identical in every way with the true, still depends on it through the ends aimed at by the will. There is, therefore, between the two, a bond more or less loose or close, but unbreakable.

It is not by the individuality in us that we approach truth; it is in virtue of a participation in the universal. This universal, which is at one and the same time the true and the good, cannot be honored as the true—we cannot enter into intimate union with it, discover its traces, and yield ourselves to its mighty sway—unless we recognize and serve it equally as the good.

Climb up the Great Pyramid by those giant steps that so exactly represent the ascent of the true: if you go up by the northern edge, can you reach the summit without getting nearer and nearer to the southern edge? To keep away from it would be to stay on the low levels; to turn away from it would be to go sideways and downwards. Similarly the genius of the true tends of itself to join the good; if it diverges it is at the expense of its upward impulse towards the summits.

Blessed are the pure of heart, said the Lord, they shall see God. "Preserve purity of conscience," says St. Thomas to his student; "do not fail to imitate the conduct of the saints and of good men." Responsiveness of the soul to the ineffable spring, its filial and loving dispositions, lay it open to receive light after light, and ever-increasing fervor and rectitude. Truth, when loved and realized as a life, shows itself to be a first principle; one's vision is according to what one is; one participates in truth by participating in the Spirit through whom it exists. Great personal intuitions, piercing lights, are in men of equal powers the consequence of moral progress, of detachment from self and from the usual commonplace things, of humility, simplicity, discipline of the senses and the imagination, of an eager impulse towards the great ends.

There is no question now of proving one's skill, of showing off the brilliance of one's powers, as of a jewel; one desires to get into communion with the radiant center of light and life; one approaches this center in its unity, as it is; one adores it, and renounces what is opposed to it in order to be flooded with its glory. Is not all that something like the meaning of the famous words: "Great thoughts come from the heart"? [1]

II

We see then that virtue in general is necessary for knowledge, and that the more moral rectitude

[1] One of Pascal's *Pensées*. In Pascal's language *coeur* means the whole man, with his experience, perceptions, intuitions (Tr. Note).

we bring to study, the more fruitful the study is. Yet there is a virtue proper to the intellectual, and we must dwell on it here, although it will recur often in the course of these pages.

The virtue proper to the man of study is, clearly, studiousness. Do not jump to the conclusion that this is a naïve statement: our masters in doctrine have included many things in that virtue, and have distinguished from it many other things.[1]

St. Thomas placed studiousness under the heading of the controlling virtue of temperance, to indicate that of itself, knowledge is no doubt always to be welcomed, but that our life is so ordered as to require us to temper, that is, to adapt to circumstances and to reconcile with other duties, a thirst for knowing that may easily run to excess.

When I say to excess, I mean in both directions. To the virtue of studiousness, two vices are opposed: negligence on the one hand, vain curiosity on the other. We shall not speak here of the former; if it is not hateful to the reader when he comes to close this little book, it will be because he has grown weary on the way, or because we have managed the journey very badly. It is not the same with curiosity. This fault can creep in under cover of our best instincts, and vitiate them at the very moment that it pretends to satisfy them.

We have already referred to the ambitious ideas which pervert an intellectual vocation. Without going as far as that, ambition may injure studiousness, and hinder the usefulness of its results. An act

[1] St. Thomas, Summa Theologica, 2a, 2ae, qu. 167.

of ambition apropos of knowledge ceases to be an act of the pursuit of knowledge, and he who indulges in it ceases to deserve the name of an intellectual.

Every other faulty purpose would call for the same verdict.

On the other hand, study, even when it is disinterested and right in itself, is not always opportune; if it is not, the person who then pursues knowledge forgets his duty as a man, and what is to be said of the intellectual who is not a man?

Other duties than study are human duties. Knowledge taken in an absolute sense is no doubt our supreme good, but the modicum of it that is granted to us here is often subordinated to other values which, in regard of merit, will be its equivalent.

A country priest who devotes himself to his parishioners, a doctor who turns away from study to give help in urgent cases, a young man of good family who adopts a calling to help his people and in doing so has to turn his back on liberal studies, are not profaning the gift that is in them, they are paying homage to the True which is one and the same Being with the Good. If they acted otherwise they would offend truth no less than virtue, since, indirectly, they would be setting living truth at variance with itself.

One sees many men avid for knowledge who do not hesitate to sacrifice to it their strictest duties. They are not men of study, they are dilettanti.

Or else they abandon the study demanded by their obligations and take up some other that flatters their inclination, and their loss of quality is the same.

Those who aim at what is beyond their powers, and thus run the risk of falling into error, who waste their real capacity in order to acquire some capacity that is illusory, are also men of curiosity in the olden sense. Two of St. Thomas's sixteen precepts for study concern them: *"Altiora te ne quaesieris,* do not seek what is beyond your reach." *"Volo ut per rivulos, non statim, in mare eligas introire;* I want you to decide to go to the sea by the streams, not directly." Precious advice, which serves knowledge as well as virtue by giving balance to the man.

Do not overload the foundation, do not carry the building higher than the base permits, or build at all before the base is secure: otherwise the whole structure is likely to collapse.

What are you? What point have you reached? What intellectual substructure have you to offer? These are the things that must wisely determine your undertaking. "If you want to see things grow big, plant small," say the foresters; and that is, in other words, St. Thomas's advice. The wise man begins at the beginning, and does not take a second step until he has made sure of the first. That is why self-taught men have so many weak points. They cannot, all by themselves, begin at the beginning. When they join a group already well on the road, they find themselves at a stage where other stages have already been passed, and there is no one to show them the approaches.

On the other hand, what is true of each one as to the stages of his development is true of each one in relation to others. We must not overestimate ourselves, but we must judge of our capacity. To accept ourselves as we are is to obey God and to make sure of good results. Does nature seek to exceed her powers? Everything in nature is exactly measured, without vain effort and without false estimates. Every creature acts according to its quantity and quality, its nature and its power, and then is at peace. Man alone lives in pretentiousness and dissatisfaction.

What wisdom and what virtue there is in judging oneself truly and in remaining oneself! You have a part that only you can play; and your business is to play it to perfection, instead of trying to force fortune. Our lives are not interchangeable. Equally by aiming too high and by falling too low, one misses the path to the goal. Go straight ahead, in your own way, with God for guide.

To this necessary prudence St. Thomas adds the importance of not letting one's curiosity linger over earthly objects at the expense of the supreme object. Later on we shall draw from that a consequence which is important for the organization of our work; [1] but study must first of all leave room for worship, prayer, direct meditation on the things of God. Study is itself a divine office, an indirect

[1] Cf. below: The Field of Work: Comparative Study.

divine office; it seeks out and honors the traces of the Creator, or His images, according as it investigates nature or humanity; but it must make way at the right moment for direct intercourse with Him. If we forget to do this, not only do we neglect a great duty, but the image of God in creation comes between us and Him, and His traces only serve to lead us far from Him to whom they bear witness.

Study carried to such a point that we give up prayer and recollection, that we cease to read Holy Scripture, and the words of the saints and of great souls—study carried to the point of forgetting ourselves entirely, and of concentrating on the objects of study so that we neglect the Divine Dweller within us, is an abuse and a fool's game. To suppose that it will further our progress and enrich our production is to say that the stream will flow better if its spring is dried up.

The order of the mind must correspond to the order of things. In the world of reality, everything rises towards the divine, everything depends on it, because everything springs from it. In the effigy of the real within us, we can note the same dependence, unless we have turned topsy-turvy the true relations of things.

III

These dispositions will be secured, if apart from the exercises of piety which precede our study, we cultivate in work itself the spirit of prayer.

It is again St. Thomas who tells the passionate seeker after knowledge: *"Orationi vacare non desinas:* never give up praying," and Van Helmont explains this precept when he says these sublime words: "Every study is a study of eternity."

We repeat continually that science (*scientia*) is knowledge by causes. Details are nothing: facts are nothing: the important things are the dependences, the transmissions of influence, the connecting links, the exchanges, which constitute the life of nature. Now, behind all these dependences, is the primal dependence; at the spot to which all connections converge is the supreme Bond; at the highest point of all transmissions, the Spring; beneath the exchanges the Gift; beneath the systole and diastole of the world, the Heart, the boundless Heart of Being. Must not the mind refer back to it unceasingly, and never for a minute lose touch with what is thus the All of all things, and consequently of all knowledge?

Intelligence only plays its part fully when it fulfils a religious function, that is, when it worships the supreme Truth in its minor and scattered appearances.

Each truth is a fragment which does not stand alone but reveals connections on every side. Truth in itself is one, and the Truth is God.

Every truth is a reflection; behind the reflection, and giving it value, is the Light. Every being is a witness; every fact is a divine secret; beyond them is the object of the revelation, the hero witnessed to. Everything true stands out against the Infinite as against its background; is related to it; belongs to it. A particular truth may indeed occupy the stage, but there are boundless immensities beyond. One might say a particular truth is only a symbol, a symbol that is real, a sacrament of the absolute; it is a sign, and it exists, but not of itself; it does not stand of itself; it lives by what it borrows and would die if left to its own unsubstantiality.

Hence, for the fully awakened soul, every truth is a meeting-place; the sovereign Thought invites ours to the sublime meeting; shall we miss it?

The life of the real is not entirely in what we see, in what we can analyze by knowledge. The real has a hidden life, like Jesus, and this life also is a life in God; it is, as it were, a life of God; it is a revelation of His wisdom in laws, of His power in effects, of His goodness in the usefulness of things, of His tendency to diffuse Himself in exchange and growth; it is a kind of incarnation which we must venerate and love, keeping in contact with Him who thus embodies Himself. To separate this "body of God" from His Spirit is to abuse it; just as it is an abuse of Christ to see in Him the man only.

The Incarnation of Christ leads up to Communion, in which the Body, Blood, Soul, and Divinity of the Saviour are not separated; the quasi-incarnation of God in being, of eternal Truth in every separate instance of the truth, should also lead up to a heavenly ecstasy,[1] instead of our absent-minded investigations, and commonplace feelings of admiration.

Let us make up our minds to work under the

[1] See page ix of Preface, and pages 133, 255.

protective wing of the great laws and under the Supreme Law. Neither knowledge, nor any other manifestation of life, should be separated from its roots in the soul and in reality—where the God of the heart and the God of heaven are revealed and are one. Unity must be established among our acts (including the act of learning) and our thoughts, and our primal realities. In everything let us have the whole soul, the whole of nature and of duration, and Divinity itself with us.

We must add that to attain this spirit of prayer in study, it is not necessary to give oneself up to any mysterious incantation. No extrinsic effort is required. It is true that to call on God and to invoke His special intervention is in place here. St. Thomas always prayed before dictating or preaching; he composed an admirable prayer for this use: [1] the child in knowledge, stammering in his effort at expression, most naturally looks to find the word he wants in the glance of God. But in knowledge itself, in Christian knowledge, we have the stepping-stool which raises us a little towards God, so that we return to study with soul enlightened and in a sense with the gifts of the prophet.

Everything that instructs us leads to God on a hidden byway. Every authentic truth is in itself eternal, and its quality of eternity turns us towards the eternity of which it is the revelation. Through nature and the soul, where can we go if not towards

[1] Cf. *Les Prières de saint Thomas d'Aquin;* Art Catholique, Paris.

their origin? If one does not get there, it is because one has gone off the path. At one bound the inspired and right mind goes beyond intermediaries, and to every question that arises within it, whatever particular answers it may make, a secret voice says: God!

Therefore, we have only to leave the mind on the one hand to its upward flight, on the other to its attention, and there will be set up, between the object of a particular study and the object of religious contemplation, an alternating movement which will profit both. With a rapid and often unconscious impulse, we pass from the trace or the image to God, and then, coming back with new vigor and strength, we retrace the footsteps of the divine Walker. We now find things have a deeper meaning, are magnified; we see in them an episode of an immense spiritual happening. Even while we busy ourselves with some trifling thing, we feel ourselves dependent on truths in comparison with which the mountains are ephemeral; infinite Being and infinite duration enfold us, and our study is in very truth, "a study of eternity."

IV

We have already said that the doctrine of the composite nature of man forbids us to dissociate spiritual functions from even those corporal functions that are apparently least connected with pure thought. St. Thomas subscribes to this ironical notion of Aristotle: It is as ridiculous to say, the soul alone understands, as to say, alone it builds or weaves.[1] He himself advances the following propositions which look materialistic: "The different dispositions of men for the operations of the soul depend on the different dispositions of their bodies." [2] "To a good bodily constitution corresponds the nobility of the soul." [3]

That need not surprise us. Thought is born in us after long processes of preparation in which the whole bodily machine is at work. The chemistry of the cell is the basis of everything; the most obscure sensations prepare our experience; this experience is the product of the work of the senses, which slowly elaborate their acquisitions and fix them through memory. It is amid physiological phenomena, in continuity with them and in dependence on them, that the intellectual operation takes place. No one thinks, even if he is only utilizing an acquired idea, without calling up a whole complex of images, emotions, sensations, which are the culture medium of the idea.

When we want to awaken a thought in anyone, what are the means at our disposal? One only, to produce in him by word and sign states of sensibility and of imagination, emotion, and memory in which he will discover our idea and make it his own. Minds can only communicate through the body. Similarly, the mind of each one of us can only communicate with truth and with itself

1 Q.XIX *de Veritate,* art. 1, arg. 1.
2 *De Memoria,* lect. 1.
3 In II *De Anima,* lect. 19.

through the body. So much so, that the change by which we pass from ignorance to knowledge must be attributed, according to St. Thomas, directly to the body and only accidentally to the intellectual part of us.[1]

Should not this doctrine, continually recurring in the Master's teaching, and so essentially, so providentially modern, engender the conviction that in order to think, and especially in order to think ardently and wisely throughout a lifetime, it is indispensable to subject to the requirements of thought not only the soul and its various faculties, but also the body and the whole complex of its organic functions? In an intellectual, everything must be intellectual. The physical and mental composite, the substance man, are at the service of that special life which in some aspects seems hardly human: let them place no hindrances in the way! Let us make ourselves a harmony of which the result will be the conquest of the true.

Now, there are here two considerations that must be faced without any human respect, although the first customarily startles spiritual persons who lack firmness of judgment.

First then, do not be ashamed to endeavor to keep well.

Some men of genius have had miserably bad health, and if it is God's will that that should happen to you, there is no more to be said. But if it is your own fault, it is a very guilty instance of tempting God. Are you quite sure that, following the ex-

[1] St. Thomas, Q.XXVI *de Veritate* art. 3, ad 12m.

ample of men of genius, you will, like them, have enough vigor to triumph in the incessant struggle of the soul against the weakness of the flesh? There is no proof that these great men themselves have not had their talents turned astray or dimmed by their physiological defects. Many intellectual anomalies in the most gifted might perhaps be thus explained, and so might the limited production of some among them.

In men of otherwise equal gifts, it is certain that sickness is a serious handicap. It lessens the output; it interferes with the freedom of the soul at the moment of its delicate operations; it sidetracks attention; it may warp the judgment by the effects on imagination and the nervous reactions that suffering brings about. A disease of the stomach changes a man's character, his character changes his thoughts. If Leopardi had not been delicate and deformed, would he have been among the pessimists?

When, therefore, you resolve to live on a high level, do not imagine that it is taking a low stand to consider carefully, along with the activity of thought itself, all the particulars of its organic substructure. "A sound mind in a sound body" remains the ideal. The thinker has a special physiology; he must look after it and not hesitate to take expert advice on the matter.[1]

In any case, ordinary current rules must be

[1] Cf. Réveillé Parise: *Physiologie et hygiène des hommes livrés aux travaux de l'esprit,* 1881.

obeyed. Sound hygiene is almost, for you, an intellectual virtue. Among our moderns, whose philosophy is sometimes so poor, the science of hygiene is rich; do not despise it; it will enrich your philosophy.

Live as much as possible in the open air. It is a recognized fact that attention—the nerve of study—is closely related to breathing, and for general health we know that plenty of oxygen is a first condition. Windows open or partly open day and night when prudence allows, frequent deep breathing exercises, combined with movements that amplify them and make them normal, walks before and after work or even combined with work according to the Greek tradition; all these practices are excellent.

It is important to work in a position that gives free play to the lungs and does not compress the other organs. It is good from time to time to interrupt a spell of close application in order to breathe deeply, to stretch one's limbs in two or three rhythmic movements which relax the body and even prevent it from getting wrinkles. It has been found that slow and deep breaths, taken standing on tiptoe, with the window open, are still more effective as a relaxing agent. Neglect nothing where your health is concerned.

Every day you should take exercise. Remember the saying of an English doctor: "Those who do not find time to take exercise must find time to be ill." If you cannot take exercise in the open air, there are excellent substitute methods. That of J. P. Muller is one of the most intelligent; [1] and there are others.

For a change some easy manual work is precious both for mind and body. Our fathers knew that; but our age is a mad age that mocks at nature, and nature takes her revenge. Set aside every year, and secondarily in the course of the year, time for real vacations. By which I do not mean the entire absence of work—that would relax to excess faculties already sufficiently inclined to instability—but the predominance of rest, fresh air, and exercise out-of-doors.

Look after your diet. Light food, plain, moderate in quantity and simply cooked, will enable you to work more freely and alertly. A thinker does not spend his life in the processes of digestion.

Pay still more attention to your sleep. Take neither too much nor too little. Too much will make you heavy, stupid, will slow up the blood and the power of thinking; too little will expose you to the risk of prolonging unduly the stimulation of work and dangerously superimposing strain upon strain. Watch yourself; in this question of sleep, as in that of food, find out how much you need and make a firm resolution to keep to it. There is no general rule.

To sum up, you must understand that, for an intellectual, care of the body, which is the instrument of the soul, is virtue and wisdom; St. Thomas

[1] J. P. Muller: *Mon système* (Ed. Lafitte).

explicitly attributes this character to it, and includes this wisdom for the body among the elements that contribute to temporal beatitude, the first beginning of the other beatitude.[1] Do not turn into a wizened and stunted creature, a failure, who later on might be dull-witted, an old man before his time, and therefore a foolish steward of the talent entrusted to him by the Master.

But the care of our bodily partner includes other elements also. We have spoken of the passions and vices as formidable enemies of the mind. We were thinking then of their psychological effects, of the disturbance that they cause in the judgment, and in the habitual tendency of the mind, which, when they reach a certain degree, they turn into a power of darkness. Now we are considering their physical effects, which indirectly are again diseases of the soul.

If one remains lazy, a glutton, a slave of the pillow and of the table; if one abuses wine, alcohol, tobacco; if one forgets oneself among unwholesome excitements, clinging to habits that are both debilitating and nerve-exhausting, to sins that are perhaps periodically forgiven, but of which the effects remain, how can one practice the hygiene of which we have urged the necessity?

A lover of pleasure is an enemy of his body and therefore quickly becomes an enemy of his soul. Mortification of the senses is necessary for thought, and can alone bring us to that *state of clear vision*

[1] *Contra Gentes,* III, cap. cxli.

of which Gratry spoke. If you obey the flesh, you are on the way to become flesh, whereas you must become all spirit.

Why is St. Thomas called the Angelic Doctor? Is it only because of his winged genius? No, it is because everything in him was subordinated to his brilliant and holy mind, because his flesh, native to the coasts of the Tyrrhenian Sea, had taken on the whiteness of Carmel and Hermon; because, being chaste, temperate, quick to follow his soaring inspiration, and far from all excess, he was wholly a soul, "an intelligence served by organs," according to the famous definition.

I say to you, Catholic workers, and especially to you young men, that discipline and mortification of the body, along with the necessary care of it, of which, in themselves, they form the better part, are among the most precious safeguards of your future.

chapter 3

The Organization of Life

I

In order that everything in you should be directed towards your work, it is not enough to organize yourself within, definitely to settle your vocation and to make wise use of your powers; you must further arrange your exterior life, I mean in respect of its framework, its obligations, its contacts, its setting.

One word suggests itself here before any other: you must *simplify* your life. You have a difficult journey before you—do not burden yourself with too much baggage. Perhaps you are not absolutely free to do this, and so you think there is no use laying down rules. That is a mistake. Given the same external circumstances, a desire for simplification can do much, and what one cannot get rid of outwardly, one can always remove from one's soul.

"Thou shalt not plow with an ox and an ass together" says the Law: wise and peaceful work must not be associated with the noisy and spasmodic interruptions of a life all on the outside. Under this form again a certain asceticism is the duty of the thinker. Contemplation, whether religious or secular, scientific, artistic, or literary, is not compatible with the complications and burdens of an excessively comfortable life. "Big men have little beds," notes Henri Lavedan. There is a luxury tax to be paid on intellectual greatness. Our talent will not be ruined by the ten per cent which is the price of our privilege. The tax is paid, rather, by our faults, and certainly by our temptations; and this brings us a double advantage.

If you want to entertain knowledge as your guest, you do not need rare furniture, nor numerous servants. Much peace, a little beauty, certain conveniences that save time, are all that is necessary.

Slacken the tempo of your life. Receptions, visits that give rise to fresh obligations, formal intercourse with one's neighbors, all the complicated ritual of an artificial life that so many men of the world secretly detest—these things are not for a worker. Society life is fatal to study. Display and dissipation of mind are mortal enemies of thought. When one thinks of a man of genius, one does not imagine him dining out.

Do not let yourself get entangled in that mesh of occupations which little by little monopolizes time, thought, resources, powers. Conventions must not dictate to you. Be your own guide; obey your convictions, not mere custom; and the convictions of an intellectual must correspond to the goal at which he is aiming.

Vocation means concentration. The intellectual is consecrated; let him not scatter himself in exacting futilities. Let him throw all his resources into the fire of inspiration, as Bernard Palissy sacrificed his furniture. The work and the conditions that further it are the whole thing. Money and attention squandered on trifles would be much better spent in collecting a library, providing for instructive travel or restful holidays, going to hear music which rekindles inspiration, and so on.

Whatever furthers your work is always timely; what impedes it and entangles you is to be put away, for, besides the immediate drawbacks, you are thus driven to work for profit and you deflect your effort. The priest has the right to live by the altar and the man of study by his work; but one does not say Mass for money and one must not think and write for money.

Suppose you are of the number of those who have to earn their living otherwise than by the work they love, how will you preserve the few hours at your disposal if your life is over-full? You must reduce matter to the minimum, so as to lighten and liberate the spirit.

In this respect the wife of an intellectual has a mission that it is perhaps well to point out; it so often happens that she forgets it, and, instead of being Beatrice, succeeds in being merely a spendthrift and a chatterbox.

Every woman should espouse the career of her husband; the father's toil is always the center of gravity of the family. In that is productive life, and therefore also essential duty. And this is all the truer as the career embraced is nobler and more laborious. In such a case life in common centers round something very lofty; the wife should take her stand on the height, instead of trying to draw the man's thought down from it. To draw the husband into trivial things that have no connection with his aspirations is to rouse in him an equal aversion for both these contradictory lives. Let the daughter of Eve think of this and not give more cause than is just for St. Paul's *"divisus est."* If the married man is in a certain sense divided let him also be doubled. God has given him a helpmate like unto himself; let her not become different. The friction caused by lack of understanding in the sister soul is fatal to production; it keeps the mind in gnawing disquiet; it destroys all its soaring eagerness and all its joy; and how could the bird fly without its wings; how could bird or soul fly without their song?

Let the guardian spirit of the hearth be not its evil genius, but its muse. Having married a vocation, let her have the vocation also. Whether she achieve something herself or through her husband, what does it matter? She must still achieve since she is but one flesh with him who achieves. Without needing to be herself an intellectual, still less a woman of letters or a bluestocking, she can produce much by helping her husband to produce, compelling him to keep a watch on himself, to give of his best; helping him to recover after the inevitable lapses, buoying him up when he loses courage, consoling him for his disappointments without accentuating them through undue insistence, soothing his sorrows, being his sweet reward after his labors.

After the effort of work, a man is like a wounded soldier. He needs to be surrounded with care and quiet; do not force him, let him relax and encourage him, take an interest in what he is doing; add your strength to his at the moment that he is, as it were, depleted by a perhaps excessive expenditure of himself; in short, be a mother to him, and this strong man, who is all weakness, will feel himself braced up and fresh for new struggles.

Children complicate life, but so sweetly that they should serve to give the worker fresh courage rather than to lessen his resources. The little ones take much of you, and what good would they be if they did not now and then tease and tax you? But they hearten you just as much, and perhaps more; they can heighten your inspiration by mingling joy with it; they give you a love-lit reflection of nature and of man and thus defend you against the abstract; they bring you back to the real, about which their questioning eyes are waiting for an exact commentary from you. Their pure faces preach integrity, that sister of knowledge; and does not their readiness to believe, to hope, to have great dreams, and to expect everything from the fatherhood that guides them—does not this uplift you also, you man of thought, and give you a motive for hope? You can see an image of God and a sign of our immortal destiny in this image of the future.

Those who have renounced family life in order to devote themselves entirely to their work and to Him who inspires it have the right to rejoice, appreciating the freedom procured them by their sacrifice. They will think of their brethren laden with responsibilities and repeat to themselves the smiling remark of Lacordaire about Ozanam: "There is one snare that he did not succeed in avoiding, marriage." But the worker bound by these ties can and must draw from them strength, inspiration, and one of the forms of his ideal.

II

In the organization of our life, the essential point to safeguard, in view of which all the rest is necessary, is the wise provision of solitude, exterior and interior. St. Thomas is so deeply convinced of this that of sixteen counsels to the intellectual, he devotes seven to external contacts and to the retired life. "I want you to be slow in speaking and slow in going to the parlor." "Do not inquire at all about the actions of others." "Be polite to everyone" but "be familiar with none, for too much familiarity breeds contempt and gives matter for many distractions." "Do not busy yourself about the words and actions of those in the world." "Avoid useless outings above everything." "Love your cell, if you desire to be admitted to the wine-cellar."

The wine-cellar mentioned here, in an allusion to the *Canticle of Canticles* and to the commentary of St. Bernard, is the secret dwelling-place of truth, of which from afar the perfume attracts the spouse, that is the fervent soul; it is the abode of inspiration, the radiant center of enthusiasm, of genius, of invention, of ardent search; it is the scene of the activity of the mind and its wise delight.

To enter into that dwelling, we must give up commonplace things; we must practice retirement, of which the monastic cell is the symbol. "In the cells, and along the great corridors," writes Paul Adam (*Dieu,* p. 67), "silence is like a splendid person, clad in the whiteness of the walls, keeping watch." What does she keep watch over, if not prayer and work?

Therefore, be slow to speak and slow to go to those places where people speak, because in many words the spirit is poured out like water; by your amiability to all, purchase the right really to frequent only a few whose society is profitable; avoid, even with these, the excessive familiarity which drags one down and away from one's purpose; do not run after news that occupies the mind to no purpose; do not busy yourself with the sayings and doings of the world, that is with such as have no moral or intellectual bearing; avoid useless comings and goings which waste hours and fill the mind with wandering thoughts. These are the conditions of that sacred thing, quiet recollection. Only in this way does one gain access to the royal secrets which are the happiness of the Spouse; only by this mode of living does one hold oneself respectfully face to face with truth.

Retirement is the laboratory of the spirit; interior solitude and silence are its two wings. All great works were prepared in the desert, including the redemption of the world. The precursors, the followers, the Master Himself, all obeyed or have to obey one and the same law. Prophets, apostles, preachers, martyrs, pioneers of knowledge, inspired artists in every art, ordinary men and the Man-God, all pay tribute to loneliness, to the life of silence, to the night.

In the primeval night and its solemn emptiness the universe was shaped by the creative hand. He who desires the joy of creating must not be in a hurry to pronounce his *fiat lux,* nor especially to pass in review all the animals in the world; in propitious darkness let him take time, like God, to prepare the material of the stars.

The most exquisite songs in nature are heard at night. The nightingale, the crystal-voiced toad, the cricket, sing in the darkness. The cock proclaims the day, and does not wait for it. All who bear a message, all poets, all seekers also and those who are on the alert to pick up the truths that lie scattered round us, must plunge deep into the vast emptiness which is plenitude.

No great man has tried to escape this law. Lacordaire said that he had made for himself in his room between his soul and God "a horizon wider than the world"; and had procured for himself "the wings of rest." Emerson proclaimed himself "a savage." Descartes shut himself up in his "heated room." Plato declared that he used "more oil in his lamp than wine in his goblet." Bossuet would get up at night to find the genius of silence and inspiration; great thoughts came to him only when he was far from futile noises and preoccupations. Has not every poet the impression that in his verses he is but translating the mysterious revelations of silence, which according to the formula of Gabriele d'Annunzio he hears as "a voiceless hymn"?

The things that count must set up a barrier between him and the things that do not count. Commonplace life and the *ludibria* that St. Augustine spoke of, the games and the quarrels of children ending in a kiss, must cease under the kiss of the muse, under the delight-giving and tranquilizing caress of truth.

"Why hast thou come?" St. Bernard asked himself about the cloister: *ad quid venisti?* And you, thinker, why have you come to this life outside the ordinary life, to this life of consecration, concentration, and therefore of solitude? Was it not because of a choice? Did you not prefer truth to the daily lie of a scattered life, or even to the noble but secondary preoccupations of action? That being so, will you be unfaithful to the object of your devotion by falling back into the grip of what you have freely given up?

If the Spirit is to lead us into the regions of interior solitude, as He led Jesus into the desert, we must first offer Him the solitude we have created. Without retirement, there is no inspiration. But within the circle of the lamplight, the stars of thought gather above us, as it were in a firmament.

When silence takes possession of you; when far from the racket of the human highway the sacred fire flames up in the stillness; when peace, which is the tranquility of order, puts order in your thoughts, feelings, and investigations, you are in the supreme disposition for learning; you can bring your materials together; you can create; you are definitely at your working point; it is not the moment to dwell on wretched trifles, to half live while time runs by, and to sell heaven for nothings.

Solitude enables you to make contact with yourself, a necessity if you want to realize yourself—not to repeat like a parrot a few acquired formulas, but to be the prophet of the God within you who speaks a unique language to each man.

We shall come back later, at length, to this idea of an equipment special to each person, of a mental training which is education, that is, the drawing-out and unfolding of a soul: a soul that is unique, that has not had nor will have its like in all the ages, for God does not repeat Himself. But we must bear in mind that one can only unfold oneself in that fashion by first living with oneself, closely, in solitude.

The author of the *Imitation* said: "I have never gone amongst men without coming back less a man." Carry that idea further and say: without coming back less the man that I am, less myself.

In the crowd one loses one's identity, unless one keeps firm hold of oneself, and this hold must first be created. In the crowd, one has no self-knowledge, being burdened by an alien self, that of the multitude.

"What is thy name?—Legion." That would be the answer of your spirit dispersed and scattered in the life outside you.

Hygienists recommend three things for the body: the bath, the air bath, and the inward bath of pure water; I should like to add for the soul the bath of silence, in order to tone up the organism of the spirit, to accentuate the personality, and to produce the active consciousness of it, as the athlete feels his muscles and prepares their play by the inner movements which are their very life.

Ravignan said: "Solitude is the homeland of the strong, silence is their prayer." What a prayer indeed there is to truth, and what a power of cooperation with its influence in prolonged recollection—frequently resumed at specified times, as it were for a meeting which will gradually become a continuous contact, a life in close community! One cannot, says St. Thomas, contemplate all the time; but he who lives only for contemplation, directs everything else towards it, and resumes it when he can, gives it a sort of continuity, as far as may be on earth.[1]

Delight will be found in it, for "the cell, if you stay in it, grows sweet: *cella continuata dulcescit.*" Now the delight of contemplation is a part of its

[1] S.T. 1a 2ae, qu. 3, art. 2 ad 4m.

efficacy. Pleasure, St. Thomas explains, fastens the soul to its object, like a vise; it rivets attention and liberates the acquisitive faculties, which sadness or boredom would constrain. When truth takes possession of you and slips her downy wing beneath your soul to lift it gently and harmoniously in upward flight, that is the moment to rise with her and to float, as long as she supports you, in the upper air.

You will not thereby live in the isolation that we have condemned; you will not be far from your brethren because you have left their noise behind you—the noise which separates you from them spiritually, and therefore prevents true brotherhood.

For you, an intellectual, your neighbor is the person who needs the truth, as the neighbor of the good Samaritan was the wounded man by the wayside. Before giving out truth, acquire it for yourself; and do not waste the seed for your sowing.

If the words of the *Imitation* are true, you will be more a man and more with men when you are far from them. In order to know humanity and to serve it, we must enter into ourselves, where all the objects we pursue are together in contact, and get from us either our strength of truth or our power of love.

One can only achieve union with anything through interior liberty. To allow oneself to be possessed, to be pulled hither and thither, whether by people or by things, is to promote disunion. Out of sight, near the heart.

Jesus shows us truly that one can be entirely recollected, and entirely devoted to others—entirely given to men and living entirely in God. He preserved His solitude: He touched the crowd only with a soul of silence, to which His words were like a narrow doorway for the interchanges of divine charity. What sovereign efficacy there was in that contact which reserved everything except the precise point through which God could pass and souls reach Him!

The fact is that there would be no place between God and the multitude, except for the Man-God and for the man of God, the man of truth, who is ready to give. He who thinks himself united with God without being united with his brothers is a liar, says the apostle; he is but a false mystic, and, intellectually, a false thinker; but he who is united to men and to nature without being hiddenly united to God—without being a lover of silence and solitude—is but the subject of a kingdom of death.

III

All our explanations so far show clearly that the solitude we have extolled is a value needing to be modified by related values, which complete it and turn it to account. We are not pleading for a solitude without a purpose. The sacrifice of intercourse with our brethren and of their sympathy carries a compensation. The retirement to which we have a right must be a splendid isolation. Now, will it not be all the richer, all the more fruitful if the higher contacts which we seek in retirement are furthered by consorting in wise measure with well-chosen associates?

The first association of the intellectual, that which will show him for what he is—apart of course from his needs and his human duties—is association with his fellows. I use the word association, I should prefer to say cooperation, for to associate without cooperating is not doing intellectual work. But how rare, in this age of individualism and social anarchy, is such a kinship of minds! P. Gratry deplored it: he dreamed of Port-Royal, and wanted to make of the Oratory "a Port-Royal without the schism." "What labor could be saved," he said, "if people could join and help one another! If six or seven together, with the same idea, worked by way of mutual teaching, becoming turn by turn pupil and master of the others; if by some happy concourse of circumstances they could even live together! If besides lectures in the afternoon and study following on the lectures, they could talk in the evening, at supper, of all these noble things, so as to learn more by drinking them in in conversation, than by the very lectures!" [1]

The workshops of old, especially those of the artists, were a gathering of friends, a family. The workshop of today is a jail, or a union meeting. But in response to the need which makes itself more and more felt around us, shall we not see the old comradely workshop revived, widened, opened up, and yet no less closely united than of yore? The

[1] *Les Sources*, Première partie, Ch. VII.

time would be opportune to conceive and to found the intellectual workshop or consortium, an association of workers all equally enthusiastic and diligent, banded together freely, living in simplicity, in equality, no one aiming at domination, even though someone might have a recognized superiority which would be of advantage to the group. Without pride or the spirit of rivalry, seeking only truth, the friends thus gathered together would, so to say, multiply one another, and their common soul would reveal a wealth of which no sufficient explanation would appear to be discoverable in any single part.

One needs such a strongly tempered soul to work alone! What heroism it is to be one's own intellectual society, one's own encouragement and support, to find in a poor isolated will the strength that might spring from the impetus of a multitude or from stern necessity! One begins with enthusiasm, then as some difficulty arises, the demon of laziness whispers: What is the good? Our vision of the goal grows dim; the fruit of effort is too distant or appears too bitter; we have a vague sense of being duped. It is certain that the support of others, their example, the exchange of ideas, would be admirably efficacious against this gloomy mood; they would supply the place in many people of that power of imagination and constancy of virtue which only the few possess, yet which are necessary for the persevering prosecution of a great purpose.

In monasteries where there is no talking, no visiting, the influence of a corridor in which each little room is the scene of assiduous work encourages and spurs on each ascetic; these apparently isolated cells form a hive; the silence is collective; the work is in fellowship; walls are no barrier to the concord of soul; one and the same spirit reigns over all; and in the total harmony each one's thought stands out like the motif of a symphony, supported and prolonged by the great general wave of sound. And then, when an exchange takes place, the concert grows richer: each person speaks and listens, learns and teaches, takes and gives, getting something even as he gives; and perhaps this last aspect of the cooperation is most to be envied.

Friendship is an obstetric art; it draws out our richest and deepest resources; it unfolds the wings of our dreams and hidden indeterminate thoughts; it serves as a check on our judgments, tries out our new ideas, keeps up our ardor, and inflames our enthusiasm.

We have examples of all that in our day in young groups and young Reviews, in which men of understanding and conviction assume a task and devote themselves to an idea. The *Cahiers de la Quinzaine* [1] sprang from such a desire; the *Amitié de France*, the *Revue des Jeunes*, the *Revues de Juvisy* and *du Saulchoir* are every day more and more inspired by it. In these groups the workers do not always live together, but they work with the same spirit; they concert their efforts, they criticize

[1] The remarkable periodical, 1900-1914, of Charles Péguy, one of the men who has had the finest spiritual influence on modern French thought. (Tr. Note.)

one another, they are both protected and stimulated by a setting to which an initiating idea or a great tradition gives the essential character.

Try, if you can, to join some such group, try if need be to establish one.

In any case, even if you are materially isolated, seek out in spirit the society of the friends of the true. Join their assembly, feel yourself in brotherhood with them and with all the seekers, all the creators that Christianity brings together. The Communion of Saints is not a phalanstery; nevertheless it is a unity. "The flesh"—alone—"profiteth nothing": the spirit, even alone, can do something. The unanimity which bears fruit consists not so much in being together in one place, or belonging to a group with a label, as in this: that each one should labor with the feeling that others also are laboring, that each one in his place should concentrate on the work while others also are concentrating: so that one task be accomplished, that one principle of life and activity be its guiding spirit; and that the parts of the watch, to each of which a home worker devotes his exclusive attention, be put together by God.

IV

I have also said that the solitude of the thinker does not imply neglect of his duties or forgetfulness of his needs. Certain contacts are necessary. Being necessary, they are part of our life: even of the life of an intellectual, since we do not separate the intellectual from the man. It is your task to link them with your intellectual life so that not only they will not interfere with it, but will serve it.

That is always possible. The time given to duty or to real need is never lost; the care bestowed on these things is a part of your vocation, and would be an obstacle to it only if you thought of your vocation in an abstract way, apart from Providence.

"We must not think," writes Maine de Biran in his diary, "that the only and best use of time consists in regular, continuous, and tranquil mental work. As often as we act rightly, conformably to our actual present position, we are making a good use of life."

You will not imagine that your work is of more importance than you, and that even an increase of intellectual possibilities should prevail over the achievement of your true self. Do what you ought and must; if your human perfection requires it, the different demands it makes will find their own balance. The good is the brother of the true: it will help its brother. To be where we ought to be, to do what we ought to do, disposes us for contemplation, and feeds it; it is leaving God for God, according to the saying of St. Bernard.

It is painful to have to sacrifice precious hours in visits and on business which are themselves beneath our ideal; but since after all the course of the world is made to be compatible with virtue, we must conclude that virtue, intellectual or moral, will find its profit in these things. On certain days it is only indirectly, by way of moral progress, that our intelligence will gain, in spite of its concessions to duty; in other circumstances it will gain of itself, directly.

For do not forget that in association with others, even in ordinary everyday meetings, there is something to be gleaned. Too much solitude would impoverish you. Someone wrote recently: "The difficulty of novel-writers nowadays seems to me to be this: if they do not go into society their books are unreadable, and if they do, they have no time to write." That is the tormenting question of wise measure which we meet everywhere! But novel-writer or not, you must feel that you cannot shut yourself up entirely. Monks themselves do not do it. You must keep, in view of your work, the sense of the common soul, of life, and how could you have it if, cutting yourself off from human beings, you had in mind but a dream-humanity?

The man who is too isolated grows timid, abstracted, a little odd: he stumbles along amid realities like a sailor who has just come off his ship; he has lost the sense of the human lot; he seems to look on you as if you were a "proposition" to be inserted in a syllogism, or an example to be put down in a notebook.

In the inexhaustible wealth of the real, too, we can find much to learn; we must move in it in a spirit of contemplation, not keep away from it. And in the real is not man the most important thing for us—man, the center of all things, the goal to which all things lead, the mirror of all things, inviting the thinker of every specialty to permanent comparisons?

In the measure in which we can choose, we must arrange to consort as far as possible with superior minds. The wife of an intellectual should see to that also. She should not open her house at random; her tact should be a sort of sieve; more than the society of the great world, she should esteem that of noble spirits; to so-called clever men she should prefer men of weight, well-informed, of firm judgment, knowing that in society a man passes the more surely for clever, the more he has killed his intelligence. Above all, she should not through frivolity, vanity, some unimportant question of interest, take her husband among fools.

And yet even fools have their place in serving us and completing our experience. Do not seek them out; they are there in plenty! But learn to utilize those that you do meet, intellectually, by a sort of counter test; and as a human being and a Christian by practising the virtues that intercourse with them exacts from us.

Society is a book to read, even though a commonplace book. Solitude is a masterpiece; but remember the saying of Leibnitz, who found no book so bad that he could not get something out of it. You do not think alone, just as you do not think with your intelligence alone. Your intelligence takes your other faculties into partnership; your soul uses your body; your personality, its outside contacts; all these things together make up your thinking being. Adjust its component parts to the best of your power; but turn even its weak points, such as illness, into things of value by means of some happily ingenious greatness of soul.

However, in your association with others, bear

yourself so that your mind and heart are always in control. Thus if the setting is mediocre you will be neither invaded nor contaminated by it; and if it is noble it will but accentuate in you the effects of solitude, your attachment to truth and to the lessons truth has lavished on you.

Our contacts with the outer world should be like those of the angel, who touches and remains untouched unless he wills, who gives and from whom one takes nothing away because he belongs to another world.

By moderation in speech, you will also attain that continuous recollection and that wise give and take which are so important a provision for you. To speak for the sake of what must be said, to express a timely feeling or a useful idea and then to be silent, is the secret of keeping possession of yourself while giving something to others, instead of letting your own torch go out as it lights other torches.

Besides, that is the way to give weight to one's words. Speech is weighty when one perceives silence beneath it, when it conceals and yet suggests a treasure behind the words, a treasure that it gives out little by little, as is fitting, without haste and frivolous excitement. Silence is the hidden content of the words that count. What makes the worth of a soul is the abundance of what it does not express.

V

What we have said of social contacts applies also with but little modification to action. The point is the same, to find the right balance between the life within and the life without, between silence and sound.

The intellectual vocation strictly considered is the contrary of action; the contemplative life and the active life have always been contrasted as springing from contrary thoughts and aspirations. Contemplation gathers in, action gives out; the one seeks for light, the other longs to bestow its possessions on others.

Speaking generally, we must evidently resign ourselves to this division of tasks, being glad, each of us, to praise what we do not do, to love and appreciate its fruit in others, thanks to the communion of souls. But real life does not admit of such a strict separation.

Duty may force us into action as a moment ago we saw it might into the society of our fellows; and the same principles will apply. Action regulated by conscience prepares conscience itself for the rules of truth, disposes it for recollection when the time comes, unites it to Providence, which is also a source of truth. Thought and action have the same Father.

Then, even without obligation, it is always necessary for the thinker to reserve a part of his time and of his heart for the active life. It is sometimes a small part; but in a wise man it is never totally absent. The monk works with his hands or undertakes some apostolate; the great doctor has his hospitals; the artist his exhibitions, his group, his journeys, his lectures; the writer has so many calls on him that it would be hard for him not to be drawn into some external project.

That is all good. For if in this world everything has its measure, the interior life must have its measure also. This measure demands that action should have a limit and give place to solitude, because external action disturbs the soul while silence calms it. But carried too far, silence in its turn has a disturbing effect; when all a man's powers are intensely concentrated on his thinking, he easily loses his balance, his vision of the way; a diversion is indispensable to the life of the brain; we need the soothing effect of action.

There are physiological reasons for this which I will not go into; psychological reasons are based on and even identical with them, for the soul as distinct from the body would not grow tired. But the living composite grows tired of rest as well as of exertion; it demands a balance, of which the center of gravity may move and vary from one man to another. A body too long motionless gets atrophied and nerveless; a soul which does the same wilts and broods. By carrying the cult of silence too far, one would reach the silence of death.

There is another point of view: intellectual life needs to feed on facts. One finds facts in books; but everyone knows that purely bookish knowledge is fragile; it suffers from the defect of the abstract; it loses contact and therefore sets before the judgment matter that is too fine-spun, almost illusory. "You are a captive balloon," said Amiel to himself: "see that the rope holding you to earth does not wear thin."

St. Thomas devotes an article of the *Summa* to proving the need of basing oneself on the real in order to judge, because, he says, the real is the ultimate goal of judgment; now the goal, all along the road, must light the way.[1]

Ideas are in facts, they do not live of themselves as Plato thought: this metaphysical view has practical consequences. You as a man of thought must keep in touch with what is; else the mind loses its poise. What is dreaming but thought cut off from the outer world, thought that has ceased to will? Unsubstantial dreaming is the rock of abstract thought; it must be avoided, as a cause of powerlessness and failure. Thought bases itself on facts as the foot is planted on the ground, as the cripple leans on his crutches.

The element of action we are recommending to the thinker will have the advantage of steadying his mind. It will have the further advantage of enriching it. How many experiences life offers us every day! We let them pass, but a deep thinker gathers them up and makes his treasure of them; they will gradually fill out the framework of his thought, and his general ideas will be first tested and then illustrated by living examples.

The idea in us, devoid of its elements of experience, of its phantasms,[2] is but an empty concept,

[1] Ia, qu. 84, art. 8.

[2] *Phantasm,* in scholastic language, is the image of a thing left in the imagination. (Tr. Note.)

which can no longer even be perceived. In the measure in which the phantasms are abundant the thought is full and strong. Now everywhere on its path action finds assimilable elements and "slices of life" which give form and shape to abstract ideas. It will even find an uncountable number of them, for the real is a sort of infinite which no analysis, no rational estimate can exhaust.

Put an artist in front of a tree, he will make endless sketches of it, without ever imagining that he has completely rendered what nature expresses; put him before a sketch of a tree, even a tree by Claude Lorrain or Corot, when he has conscientiously copied it he has exhausted the model.

The individual is inexpressible, said the old philosophers. The individual is the real, as opposed to the themes of the mind. By plunging through action into the real, we find new forms in the matter of our observation, as the artist at work enriches, corrects, and completes his conception.

Lastly, action not only provides us with experience, but is also a teacher of energy whose lessons have their use for a solitary. By its solicitations and its resistances, by its difficulties, reverses, successes, by the boredom and weariness it forces us to overcome, by the contradictions it unfailingly arouses; and by the fresh needs it gives rise to, it stimulates us and retempers our powers; it shakes us out of our fundamental laziness and that self-satisfied quietude which are no less inimical to thought than to practical results.

The exterior virtues will thus help the interior ones, active investigation will serve recollection; the bees' spoil will prepare the honey. Thought, sounding turn by turn the two abysses of the real and the ideal, fortified by a disciplined will, enlightened and guided by those *raisons du coeur* [1] which action incessantly involves, will be a far better tool for research, a far better arbiter of truth, than pure reason perched on Porphyry's ladder.

I should like to see our man of study steadily engaged in some enterprise not too burdensome, to which he would devote a definite amount of time —not carried away by it, and yet taking a real and hearty interest in results, which should be for him something more than the logs that people go sawing up to rest their heads. To act without throwing oneself into action is not the act of a man, and man can not find real rest or instruction or training in it. Therefore, if there are not already any demands on you, look for causes that will inspire you because they are worthwhile—movements that make for light, rehabilitation, preservation, progress; leagues for the public good, societies for defense of right and for social action, all such enterprises as demand of their man, if not his whole life, at least his whole self. Devote yourself to some such work in the moments when inspiration grants you, and even imposes on you, a leave of absence that will be to her

[1] Pascal's expression for those elements of conviction that depend on the experience of life and reality, and not on mere abstract reasoning—things known largely by instinct and intuition. (Tr. Note.)

own advantage. Then you will come back to her, and the heaven she opens to you will be all the lovelier because you have made trial of the treasures, but also of the dangers, the filth, and the rugged ways of earth.

VI

It seems to me to follow from all this that silence, retirement, the solitude useful to the thinker, are realities modified by practical considerations, but inspired by a conviction of strict necessity. It is in view of retirement, silence, and inner solitude that action and outer contacts are admissible, and by them they must be regulated. It cannot be otherwise if the intellectual is truly consecrated and if it is impossible to serve two masters.

The spirit of silence must therefore pervade the whole of life. That is what matters most of all. It is said sometimes that solitude is the mother of results. Not solitude, but the state of solitude. So much so that we could, strictly speaking, conceive an intellectual life based on two hours' work per day. But does anyone imagine that having set those two hours aside one may then act as if they did not exist? That would be a grave misconception. Those two hours are given to concentration, but the consecration of the whole life is none the less necessary.

An intellectual must be an intellectual all the time. What St. Paul suggests to the Christian: whether you eat or drink or whatsoever else you do, do all to the glory of God, must apply to the Christian in search of light. For him the true is the glory of God: he must keep it always in mind, submit to it in everything. The solitude recommended to him is not so much one of place as one of recollection; it means rising above things rather than keeping away from them; it consists in an upward-tending isolation, thanks to the surrender of self to higher things and the avoidance of frivolity, wandering ideas, fickleness, capricious fancies; it reduces to practice the *conversatio nostra in coelis* of the apostle, by lifting us and our intercourse into the heaven of spirits.

To stay in one's study, and to indulge in the interior babble, the solicitations of desire, the exultation of pride, the floodtide of thoughts that introduce within us an absorbing and discordant outside world—would that be solitude? There is a false solitude as there is a false peace. On the contrary, to go out and act through duty, or wisdom, or for the sake of that relaxation of which we shall later plead the necessity, may be a higher kind of solitude, which feeds and tones up the soul instead of depressing and weakening it.

What St. Augustine calls the "purity of solitude" may be maintained everywhere; what destroys its purity may soil even its abiding-place. "You can be in a town," wrote Plato, "like a shepherd in his hut on the top of a hill." Keep your inward inspiration, your reserve, the love of what you have devoted yourself to, have the God of truth with you, and you are alone in the midst of the universe.

chapter 4

The Time of Work

I. *Continuity of Work*
II. *The Work of Night*
III. *Mornings and Evenings*
IV. *The Moments of Plenitude*

I

We have already defined the notion of intellectual work in many ways; we must now study more closely its different conditions, and first of all the time that the thinker devotes to it.

Study has been called a prayer to truth. Now prayer, the Gospel tells us, must be uninterrupted: "We ought always to pray and not to faint" (Luke 18:1). I know that this text is capable of a modified interpretation; the sense would then be: do not spend a day, a week, any long period, without speaking to God. But our masters have taken good care not so to narrow down words of such great import; they have taken them literally, and have drawn a profound doctrine from them.

Prayer is the expression of desire; its value comes from our inward aspirations, from their tenor and their strength. Take away desire, the prayer ceases; alter it, the prayer changes; increase or diminish its intensity, the prayer soars upward or has no wings. Inversely, take away the expression while leaving the desire, and the prayer in many ways remains intact. Has a child who says nothing but looks longingly at a toy in a shop window, and then at his smiling mother not formulated the most moving prayer? And even if he had not seen the toy, is not the desire for play, innate in the child as is the thirst for movement, in the eyes of his parents a standing prayer which they grant?

We ought always to pray is the same as saying: we must always desire eternal things, the temporal things which serve the eternal, our daily bread of every kind and for every need, life in all its fulness earthly and heavenly.

Apply this commentary to the active prayer which study is, and you will arrive at a most valuable consideration. The thinker is consecrated; but he is actively engaged in thinking for a very few hours only. Carlyle said he did not believe that any man of letters devoted the fifth part of his time to literature. Since the greater part of his life is thus on a dead level or lower, the man of the heights has no choice but to come down and to accept it: what a gain for him if he need not yield entirely to these humbler necessities!

As prayer can last all the time, because it is desire and the desire is constant, why should not study last all the time, seeing that it also is desire and an invocation of the true?

The desire of knowledge defines our intelligence as a vital force. Instinctively we want to know, as we ask for bread. If the majority of men remain absorbed in more earthly longings, it is the thinker's special characteristic to be obsessed by the desire for knowledge: why not keep this desire at work, constantly at work like a stream beneath which turbines have been installed?

That can be done, and psychology and experience both tell us so. The brain is always working; the turbines that I desiderate exist, they turn, they set in motion a wheel-and-pinion system whence ideas fly like sparks from a dynamo at full pressure. The nervous processes are linked in a continuous series and no more stop than the movements of the heart or the breathing of the lungs. What do we need, in order to utilize this permanent life in the service of truth? Discipline only. The dynamos must be connected to the turbines; the turbines must be turned by the stream; the desire to know must, regularly and not intermittently, set the conscious or unconscious activity of the brain in motion.

The greater part of our nervous activity goes to waste because it is not tapped. In truth it cannot be fully turned to account, for our power over it is relative, and in trying to force the yield, one would destroy the machine. But what is possible is aimed at by very few people. Habit has great weight in this matter; wisely ordered, it acts like a second nature; and it is here that our practical advice comes in.

"Try to store everything that you can," says St. Thomas to the man of study, "in the cupboard of the mind, like one who aims at filling a vessel."

We shall return to this comparison, which might lend itself to a misunderstanding; but for the moment we are speaking of having a care to acquire knowledge, not of how to do it. The important thing for the man of truth is to understand that truth is everywhere, and that he is allowing a continuous stream to pass by him which might set his soul working.

Wisdom cries in the streets, says the Bible; she lifts her voice at the crossways; she preaches at the entry of noisy places; she makes herself heard at the gates of the city: how long, ye ignorant, will ye love your ignorance? . . . Turn . . . and I will shed my spirit upon you . . . I hold out my hand and no one hearkens. (Prov. 1:20-24.) This urgent call of truth, if it were listened to, would broaden a mind and enrich it more than laborious hours of study. These would still be necessary, but the light concentrated in them would gradually diffuse itself so as to touch almost the whole of life; a circuit would be established, bringing under the study lamp the results of disseminated thinking, and then returning to give that thinking a direction, a habitual bearing, and therefore fruitfulness.

See what happens when you want to furnish a house. Until now you never thought of furniture, so little indeed that going about the streets of Paris where every fourth shop is a collector's, you did not even see the things; the shapes did not make you stop; you did not know the tendencies of fashion, the chances of a find, the specialty of this or that district, the prices, etc. On the contrary, now that your mind is awakened by desire, everything strikes you; everything holds you; Paris is like a huge store, and you know in a week what a lifetime would not have taught you.

Truth is commoner than articles of furniture. It cries out in the streets and does not turn its back on us when we turn our backs on it. Ideas emerge from facts; they also emerge from conversations, chance occurrences, theatres, visits, strolls, the most ordinary books. Everything holds treasures, because everything is in everything, and a few laws of life and of nature govern all the rest.

Would Newton have discovered gravitation, if his attention to the real had not made him observant and ready to perceive that apples fall like worlds? The laws of gravitation of minds, sociological, philosophical, moral, artistic laws, apply no less universally. Every fact may give rise to a great thought. In all contemplation, even that of a fly or of a passing cloud, there is a fit occasion for endless reflection. Every light striking on an object may lead up to the sun; every road opened is a corridor to God.

Now, we could tap all that wealth if we were on the alert. If we looked at everything with an inspired spirit, we should find lessons everywhere—prophecies or confirmations, premonitory signs or consequences of truth. But most often we are not "on the spot," or not paying attention. "Everyone looks at what I am looking at," said Lamennais at Saint-Malo, as he stood on the seashore in a storm, "but no one sees what I see."

So acquire the habit of being present at this activity of the material and moral universe. Learn to look; compare what is before you with your familiar or secret ideas. Do not see in a town merely houses, but human life and history. Let a gallery or a museum show you something more than a collection of objects, let it show you schools of art and of life, conceptions of destiny and of nature, successive or varied tendencies of technique, of inspiration, of feeling. Let a workshop speak to you not only of iron and wood, but of man's estate, of work, of ancient and modern social economy, of class relationships. Let travel tell you of mankind; let scenery remind you of the great laws of the world; let the stars speak to you of measureless duration; let the pebbles on your path be to you the residue of the formation of the earth; let the sight of a family make you think of past generations; and let the least contact with your fellows throw light on the highest conception of man. If you cannot look thus, you will become, or be, a man of only commonplace mind. A thinker is like a filter, in which truths as they pass through leave their best substance behind.

Learn to listen; and listen, first, to anyone. If it is in the marketplace, as Malherbe asserted, that one learns one's language, it is also in the marketplace, that is, in everyday life, that we can learn the language of the mind. A multitude of truths arises out of the simplest conversations. The least word listened to with attention may be an oracle. A peasant at certain moments is much wiser than a philosopher.

All men are akin when they go down into their deepest selves; and if some profound impression, some return prompted by instinct or virtuous effort to original simplicity, sweeps away conventions and the passions that ordinarily conceal us from ourselves and others, the words that fall from any man's lips have a ring of the divine.

The whole of man is in every man, and we can get a deep-reaching initiation from him. Do you not feel what you could get out of that if you were a novelist? The greatest novelist is found on the doorsteps; the least at the Sorbonne or in drawing-rooms; with this difference, that the great observer, instead of mixing, holds aloof; he lives apart, on a higher level; and the least little life is for him a drama.

Now, what the novelist is looking for can be useful to all, for we all need this profound experience. The thinker is truly a thinker only if he finds in the least external stimulus the occasion of a limitless interior urge. It is his character to keep all his life the curiosity of childhood, to retain its vivacity of impression, its tendency to see everything under an aspect of mystery, its happy faculty of everywhere finding wonderment full of consequences.

However, be very specially on the watch when you have the good fortune to talk with someone who knows and who thinks. How sad it is that superior men are of so little service to those about them! In practice, they are set down as simpletons; people see in them what they have in common with others, not their own rare qualities. There is a treasure there, and the onlookers play with the key but do not open the lock. People smile sometimes at their awkwardness, at their little absent-minded oddities, and there is no harm in that; what is stupid is to assume an attitude of superiority which forgets the greatness of the man.

Men of worth are few enough not to be thus left unused. It is true that they use their own resources, and everyone uses them unconsciously; but if we know what we are doing, we can get wisdom and a stimulus from them which may decide the whole course of a life. Many saints, great captains, explorers, scholars, artists, became what they were for having met an outstanding personality and heard the ring of a soul. The echoes of that silent call went on reverberating in them to the end of their days, a persistent voice driving them onwards: they were borne on an invisible wave. The word of a great man is sometimes, like that of God, creative.

But it is an understood thing that great men are not great until after their death. The majority of people do not recognize them. Sitting beside you is perhaps a man as great as Descartes, and you do not listen to him, you do not question him, you argue with him in a carping spirit, you cut him short with trivial remarks. And if he is not quite so great, but has a fine mind, why do you allow him to bury his wealth or to carry it away in silence?

By observing and listening—I do not mention reading because we shall come back to that—you will learn to reflect, you will assimilate and adapt to your own needs what you have acquired. Great discoveries are but reflections on facts common to all. People have passed that way myriads of times and seen nothing; and one day the man of genius notices the links between what we do not know and what is every minute before our eyes. What is knowledge, but the slow and gradual cure of our blindness? It is true that our observations need to be prepared by earlier studies and solutions. One finds what one is looking for. Only to him that hath is given. That is why I spoke of an interchange between the inner light and the outer. Still the fact remains that the mind must be perpetually ready to reflect, and perpetually ready to see, to hear—to shoot the bird as it flies, like a good sportsman.

Let us be more precise, and say that this alertness of mind can be of advantage not only to our general culture but to our specialty, to our actual present study, to the work in hand. Carry your problems about with you. The hackney horse does his run and goes back to his stall; the free courser always has his nostrils to the wind.

Since truth is everywhere and all things are connected, why not study each question in contact with kindred questions? Everything should contribute to our specialty. Everything should bear witness for or against our theses. To a large extent the universe is what we make of it. The painter everywhere sees form, color, movement, expression; the architect balances masses; the musician perceives rhythm and sound; the poet finds subjects for metaphor; a thinker sees ideas in act.

We are not here advocating any narrow particularism; it is a question of method. One cannot follow up everything. While keeping an eye open for general observation, one devotes extra attention to a particular line of research and "by always thinking of it," like Newton, one gathers together the elements of the work to be produced later.

To keep a part of one's thought always expectant is the great secret. Man's mind is a ruminant. The cow looks away into the distance, chews slowly, bites off here a tuft and there a twig, takes the whole field for her own, and the horizon as well, producing her milk from the field, feeding her dim soul on the horizon.

We are taught to live in the presence of God; can we not also live in the presence of truth? Truth is, as it were, the special divinity of the thinker. Some particular truth or some object of study may be present to us every moment. Is it wise, is it normal, to leave the man of research behind in the study, to have as it were two souls: the soul of the worker and the soul of the easygoing everyday man? This dualism is not natural; it gives ground for thinking that the pursuit of the true is a business with us, instead of being a noble passion.

All things have their season, says the Bible, and I agree that we cannot avoid making a division of time; but since as a matter of fact we are always thinking, why not utilize that thought to the advantage of what we have in mind?

Someone may say that such tension is incompatible with mental health and with the conditions of life. Granted; but then it is not a question of tension, nor even, ordinarily, of actual will. I have spoken of habit; let us speak, if you prefer, of subconsciousness. Our mind has the faculty of functioning of itself if we prepare its operation ever so little, and lightly trace the outline of the channels in which its mysterious currents will flow.

If the desire for knowledge is well anchored and the passion for truth alight in you, if your conscious attention has often been brought to bear on those facts of life which are calculated to feed the flame and to satisfy the desire, then you have turned your mind into a greyhound unleashed. It has not to make any further effort; it obeys a new nature. You think as easily in a definite direction as formerly your thought wandered at random.

This direction is no doubt only approximate, and excessive strain would be absurd; but should we reject what can be done, by reason of what cannot? You have here an immense resource; you can use it by putting a little discipline into an operation that the brain is always performing, but without your intervention and without control. Regulate that operation, and let your brain also be an intellectual worker.

In practice, you will perceive that this is not in the least tiring, that on the contrary it saves a great deal of fatigue; for the unsought finds, made like that just by looking about, made simply because one has resolved and trained oneself not to be blind, those discoveries that are often happiest because spontaneous, greatly encourage the seeker; they keep him alert and joyous; he waits with delight for the hour of quiet in which he can fix and develop the newly acquired idea.

Very often one will light in that way on the transition that was hard to find, the turning-point that sitting at one's table, stopped dead at some point of view and unable to get away from it, one would have sought in vain. What had no immediate connection with the work leads to something basic in it. The toil of study is now all lit up; one sees where one is going, and one hopes soon to have such another stroke of good fortune.

This chance process corresponds to the unpredictable workings of the brain and to the obscure operation of the association of ideas. A number of laws apply here, without there being any law to regulate their application in one instance or another, at one time or another; and since the whole process takes place without us—I mean without any deliberate act of will, merely under the impression of the desire which is the soul of the thinker and which characterizes him, as play does childhood, and love, woman—it does not involve the strain that people imagine.

Does a woman out walking get tired of watching for the admiration of the passers-by; a girl of being ready for a laugh, or a little boy of frolicking? The mind on the look-out for truth through love, not through compulsion—through a tendency instinctive at first, then cultivated but cultivated lovingly, passionately—will not toil any more than these. Such a mind is at play; like a fowler with his gun, it is enjoying a useful and delightful sport; it loves its activity, and nothing is more unlike the precise and deliberate effort of the hours of concentration.

Thus the wise man, at all times and on every road, carries a mind ripe for acquisitions that ordinary folk neglect. The humblest occupation is for him a continuation of the loftiest; his formal calls are fortunate chances of investigation; his walks are voyages of discovery, what he hears and his silent answers are a dialogue that truth carries on with herself within him. Wherever he is, his inner universe is comparing itself with the other, his life with Life, his work with the incessant work of all beings; and as he comes forth from the narrow space in which his concentrated study is done, one gets the impression, not that he is leaving the true behind, but that he is throwing his door wide open so that the world may bring to him all the truth given out in its mighty activities.

II

Père Gratry insistently recommends us not to exclude from continuous work the hours of lethargy and darkness. He wants night to be made to work. This advice rests on psychology and on experience.

Sleep is a relaxing of tension; the conscious will lays down its function, ceases to trouble about living, aims at no purpose, and thus finds itself largely given over to the general condition of nature. The attitude of the sleeper is no empty symbol; he lies nearer to earth, as if he said to nature: Take me back; long enough have I held out against your powers; standing, I have combated your determinism; against the equalization of all forces which is the law of this perishable earth, I have set up the strong reaction of life; I now surrender—until the moment comes to take up the struggle afresh.

The intensity of life being thus in abeyance, the transmission belt of the human motor having passed from the free will of the individual to the free play of cosmic forces, there results a new operation which has its own laws, which follows paths unknown to clear consciousness and brings about combinations foreign to our will or to the caprices of our wide-awake moments. Our inner powers are grouped in a new way; our thoughts arrange themselves; they intersect; the energy set free by the cessation of activity is used effortlessly. To be able to take advantage of this process without dislocating its rhythm is a fresh resource for the thinker.

It is not a question of keeping awake; on the contrary, the night-walker is a bad worker; on this point we have said that we must obey the demands of general hygiene, which should be even more insistent in the case of a man of study. But sleep itself is a worker, a partner of the daily toil; we can make its forces serve us, utilize its laws, profit by that filtering process, that clarification which takes place during the self-surrender of the night.

A bit of brain-work begun, an idea just started, an idea that some interior or exterior happening had prevented from fully shaping itself or finding its natural place, is developed during the night and links up with others; do not miss this opportunity to gain something; fix, before it vanishes again into the night of the mind, this light which may help you.

How will you set about it? Sometimes no particular ingenuity is required. When you wake, you find the collaboration of sleep all performed and recorded. The work of the previous day appears to you in a clearer light; a new path, a virgin region lies before you; some relationship of ideas, of facts, of expressions, some happy comparison or illuminating image, a whole passage perhaps or a plan ready to be realized, will have surged into your consciousness. The whole is there, clear and distinct; you will only need at the right moment to utilize what Hypnos has condescended to do for you.

But ordinarily, the thing happens differently. Nature is not at our command; she goes her way; her river brings gold in its current, but we ourselves have to recover, not to allow to be engulfed, the precious deposit washed along to us in the treasure-bearing waves.

Very often, gleams of light come in a few minutes' sleeplessness, in a second perhaps; you must fix them. To entrust them to the relaxed brain is like writing on water; there is every chance that on the morrow there will be no slightest trace left of any happening.

Do better than that. Have at hand a notebook or a box of slips. Make a note without waking up too fully, without turning on the light, if possible, then fall back into the shadows. To get the thought thus off your mind will perhaps help your sleep instead of disturbing it. If you say, I will remember, I *will* remember, that determination is more likely to interfere with your rest than a quick jotting. Remember that sleep is a relaxing of the *will.*

At other times, it is in the morning, on first awaking, that the flashes come. You open your eyes, and it is as if the inner eye also opened, drawing in light from a fresh world. The earth has revolved; the heavens of the intelligence have not now the same aspect; other constellations are shining. Take a good look at this utterly new spectacle, and do not lose a moment before fixing its broad outlines; note down its leading features, its turning-points, enough to determine all the details when you have time to come back to it.

Every thinker has experienced instances of early morning lucidity that are sometimes surprising, almost miraculous. Complete treatises have thus grown fully clear, after a long and laborious series of complicated studies during which the author felt as if he were lost in a wood with no open space or vista ahead anywhere.

Inventions have come about like that. Elements scattered in the mind, old experiments or bits of information of no apparent interest have converged, and problems have been solved of themselves by a spontaneous classification of the mental images which stood for the idea of their solution.

Quick to your notebook when such a piece of good fortune befalls you. Follow up the idea as long as it keeps coming; develop it, add nothing of your own. Without any disturbing intervention, with your attention submissively fixed on nature which is thus at work, pull gently on the chain that has been formed, draw out the links, the little accessory chains that hang from them, note down the proportions, the dependences, with no consideration of style—I mean no deliberate effort at style, for it may happen that precious elements of style reveal themselves in that fashion.

When the drawer is empty and the chain of new thought seems to have been wholly drawn out of it, stop writing, but be sure for a while to keep your eyes fixed on your wealth: it may yet increase, the chain may yet develop new links, the secondary chains may become more numerous and be again subdivided. That is all so precious that not a particle must be lost. It is so much labor saved for the day. Night, collaborating loyally, has given you without your stir, a complete day of twenty-four hours—perhaps even weeks—the time that it would have taken to hammer out by deliberate effort the splendid jewel now presented to you.

However, it is not enough to take care to gather the fruit. Sleep works of itself, but it works on existing material; it creates nothing; it is skilled in combining and simplifying, in bringing things to a head, but it can only work on the findings of experience and the labor of the day. Its work must be prepared for it. To count on it means to count first of all on oneself.

Monks have the custom, as old as the devout life,

of depositing their point for meditation each evening like a seed in the furrows of the night; they hope on awaking to find the seed already softened, penetrated by the moisture of the ground and perhaps germinating: it will grow more quickly in the sunshine of reflection and of grace.

Without giving up this practice, which might well be wide-spread among Christians, one can also sow the seed of one's work in the field of night. The human soul is rich: two seeds can be planted side by side without harming each other. Call to your mind as you fall asleep—entrust to God and to your own soul—the question that is preoccupying you, the idea that is slow in developing its virtualities, or that eludes your grasp. Do not make any effort that would delay sleep. On the contrary, rest quietly in this thought: the universe is working for me; determinism is the slave of free will and will turn its millstone while I rest; I can suspend my effort; the heavens are revolving, and as they turn they set moving in my brain delicate machinery that I might put out of order; I sleep; nature keeps watch; God keeps watch, and tomorrow I shall gather a little of the fruit of their work.

In this quiet spirit, you relax completely, more than if you thought anxiously of a morrow without help, more above all than by living over again at night, as so often happens, the worries of the day—worries exaggerated by semi-unconsciousness, which poison the night and will be there again in the morning to serve you up their bitter draught.

Just as gentle and regular work can give harmony

to the day, the unconscious work of night can bring peace and keep at bay wandering imaginations, crazy fancies that are exhausting or sinful, nightmares. If you take a child gently by the hand, his turbulence subsides.

We are in no way recommending excessive strain, nor any turning of night into day. No, you must sleep; sleep renews nature and is indispensable. But we are saying that night, as night, can itself work; that it "gives counsel"; that sleep, as sleep, is a serviceable craftsman; that rest, as rest, is an additional strength. It is entirely in accordance with their nature, and not by doing violence to their proper function, that we aim at using these helps. Rest is not death; it is life, and all life bears fruit. While you yourself can gather the fruit of sleep, do not leave it to the birds of night.

III

Hence the extreme importance, for the worker as well as for the religious man, of the mornings and evenings. One cannot prepare, supervise and end the hours of rest with an attentive spirit if those that immediately precede and follow are left to chance.

The morning is sacred; in the morning our soul, refreshed, looks out on life as from a turning-point from which we see it in one view. Our destiny lies outspread before us. We resume our task; this is the moment to accept it afresh, and to confirm, by an express act, our triple vocation as men, Christians, and intellectuals.

"Philip, remember that thou art a man": these words of the Macedonian slave to his master are spoken to us by the light of day, when falling on our eyes, it also awakens the lights of the soul; "a man" I say, not in a general sense, but specified in a precise instance, a man who stands here before God, a single, unique, personality; and, no matter how unimportant he is, alone capable of filling his own proper place.

Will not this man, emerging renewed and, as it were, reborn from the hours of unconsciousness, cast a rapid glance over his life as a whole, mark the point he has reached, map out the coming day, and so start out with springing step and clear mind on a new stage of his journey?

Such will be the combined effort of the first moment of waking, of morning prayer, of meditation, and, above all, of the Mass, if one has the possibility of hearing it or the happiness of saying it.

Waking must be a *Sursum corda!* To repeat a form of prayer at that moment is an excellent practice; to say it aloud is better; for, as psychologists know, our voice has an effect of self-suggestion on us and plays towards us the part of a double. That is a "slave" that we may not neglect; he has authority from us, he is *us,* and his voice reaches us with the strange domination of one who is at once the same and different.

Children are taught "to give their heart to God"; the intellectual, a child in that respect, must in addition give his heart to truth; he must remember that he is her servant, repudiate her enemies within himself, love her enemies without, so that they may return to her, and willingly accept the efforts that for the coming day truth asks of him.

Next comes prayer. Père Gratry advises the intellectual to say Prime, which would have Compline for its pendant in the evening; and indeed there are no prayers more beautiful, more efficacious, more inspiring. The majority of liturgical prayers are masterpieces; but these are full and sweet like the rising and setting of a star. Try: you will never be able to say any other prayers. All true life is in them, all nature, and to prepare your work with them is like going out on a journey through a wide-open door flooded with sunshine.

Whatever prayer he chooses, that of the intellectual should emphasize for a moment what is especially appropriate to himself, should extract its fruit and form from it the good resolution that will be kept by Christian work.

An act of faith in the lofty truths that are the foundation of knowledge; an act of hope that God will help us to light as well as to virtue; an act of love for Him who is infinitely lovable and for those whom our study aims at bringing near to Him; the *Pater* to ask for our bread and for the food of our intelligence; an *Ave* addressed to the Woman clothed with the sun, victorious over error as over evil. In these forms of words and in others, the intellectual finds his needs expressed, reminds himself of his task; and he can, without isolating his specialty from Christian life as a whole, profit by what is providentially deposited for him in the common treasure.

Meditation is so essential to the thinker that we need not urge it anew. We have recommended the spirit of prayer: where can it get more food than in these morning acts of contemplation in which the mind, rested, not yet caught up afresh in the cares of the day, borne and lifted up on the wings of prayer, rises with ease towards those founts of truth which study draws on laboriously?

If you can hear holy Mass, or say it, will its vastness and fulness not take possession of you? Will you not see—from this other Calvary, from this Upper Room where the farewell Banquet is renewed—the whole of humanity standing round you: that humanity with which you must not lose contact, that life lit up by the words of the Savior, that poverty succored by His riches which it is your task to succor along with Him, which you must enlighten and do your part to save while saving yourself?

The Mass really puts you into a state of eternity, into the spirit of the universal Church, and in the *Ite missa est* you are ready to see a mission, a sending out of your zeal to the destitution of the mad and ignorant earth.

The morning hours thus bedewed with prayer, freshened and vivified by the breezes of the spirit, cannot fail to be fruitful; you will begin them with faith; you will go through them with courage; the whole day will be spent in the radiance of the early light; evening will fall before the brightness is exhausted, as the year ends leaving some seed in the barns for the year to come.

Evening! how little, usually, people know about making it holy and quiet, about using it to prepare for really restorative sleep! How it is wasted, polluted, misdirected!

Let us not dwell on what men of pleasure make of it: their condition is alien to ours. But look at those serious people called workers: business men, industrialists, public officials, big merchants—I speak of them in the mass. When evening comes, they lay down the reins and throw off thought, giving their minds up to the dissipation which is supposed to refresh them, dining, smoking, playing cards, talking noisily, frequenting the theatres or the music halls, gaping at the cinema, and going to bed with minds "relaxed."

Yes, indeed, relaxed; but like a violin with all its strings completely slackened. What a labor next day to tune them all up again!

I know industrialists who find their relaxation in reading Pascal, Montaigne, Ronsard, Racine. Deep in a comfortable armchair well lit from behind, beside the fire, their family around them, quiet, or in the buzz of pleasant activity, they *live* awhile after having toiled all day. This is their moment; this is the moment of the man, when the specialist has done facing up with head and heart to innumerable difficulties.

An intellectual, if he does not need this mental compensation, needs the quietness even more. His evening should be a time of stillness, his supper a light refection, his play the simple task of setting the day's work in order and preparing the morrow's. He needs his Compline—this time I take the word figuratively—to complete and to inaugurate; for every completion of the continuous work which we postulate is a beginning as well as a terminal point. We close only to open again. Evening is the connecting medium between the daily sections which taken together make a life. In the morning we shall have forthwith to start living: we must get ready in the evening, and we must prepare the night which, after its fashion, and without our intervention links together the periods of our conscious toil.

In spite of the passionate and self-interested illusion of those who maintain that a part of man must be set aside for the life of pleasure, dissipation is not rest, it is exhaustion. Rest cannot be found in scattering one's energies. Rest means giving up all effort and withdrawing towards the fount of life; it means restoring our strength, not expending it foolishly.

I know indeed that to expend is sometimes to acquire: that is true of sport, of recreation, and we shall not merely tolerate, we shall demand, such active relaxation. But that is not the normal function of the evening. For the evening there is a double rest, spiritual and physical; rest in God and rest in mother nature. Now the first comes from prayer; the other, the rest of the body, precedes the more complete rest of the night and must lead up to it.

One should give oneself up in the evening to the quietly regular activities of which night breathing is the model. The wise thing is to let the easy bent of nature assert itself, to let habit take the place of initiative, to let keen activity give way to a simple familiar routine, in a word, to cease willing up to a point so that the renunciation of night may begin. And wisdom will appear in the ordering of this less intense life, of this peaceful semi-activity. The family will have a share in it; quiet conversation will set its seal on the union of souls; there will be an exchange of the day's impressions, of plans for the morrow; views and purposes will be strengthened; the passing of the day will have its consolations; harmony will reign; and the evening be a worthy eve of the festival that every new day should be for the Christian.

The sleeper often unconsciously takes up the position that he had long ago in his mother's womb. That is a symbol. Rest is a return to our origins: the origins of life, of strength, of inspiration; it is a retempering; that is signified by our withdrawal in the evening from the world and into ourselves. Now retempering cannot possibly be attained through fussy activity; it is rather like seeking a refuge, renewing the vigor of the human spirit by peaceful concentration; it is a restoration of organic life and of holy life in us by easing off happily, by prayer, silence, and sleep.

IV

We come at length, after speaking of the preparation, and the prolongation, and the profitable interruption of work, and of rest in view of work, to the work itself properly so-called, and the time devoted to studious concentration, to full effort. Accordingly, we shall give the name of *full* moments, moments of plenitude, to these culminating periods of the duration of our intellectual life.

The greater part of this treatise has no other object than to consider how to use that time: here we are speaking only of securing it, putting it on a stable basis, preserving it, guarding the "interior cell" against all that threatens to invade it.

Seeing that the moments of our life have very unequal values, and that for each of us the adjustment of these values obeys different laws, we cannot lay down any absolute rule; but we must insist on this one thing: you must study yourself, consider what your life is, what it enables you to do, what it furthers or excludes, what of itself it suggests for the hours of intense activity.

Will these be in the morning or in the evening, or partly in the morning and partly in the evening? You alone can decide, because you alone know your obligations and your character on which the mapping-out of your days depends.

When you have only a few free hours and can place them at will, morning seems to deserve the preference. Night has renewed your strength; prayer has given you wings; peace reigns all about you and the buzzing swarm of distractions has not begun. But for certain people there may be counter-indications. If you sleep badly you may be upset and dull in the morning. Or solitude may be lacking, and then you must wait for the hours of isolation.

Whatever decision you have made, the chosen moments must be carefully secured, and you must take all personal precautions so as to use them to the fullest. You must see to it beforehand that nothing happens to crowd up, waste, shorten, or interfere with this precious time. You want it to be a time of plenitude; then shut remote preparation out of it; make all the necessary arrangements beforehand; know what you want to do and how you want to do it; gather your materials, your notes, your books; avoid having to interrupt your work for trifles.

Further, in order to keep this time for your work and to keep it really free, rise punctually and promptly; breakfast lightly; avoid futile conversations, useless calls, limit your correspondence to what is strictly necessary; gag the newspapers! These rules, which we have given as a general safeguard for the life of study, apply most of all to its intense hours.

If you have so foreseen and settled everything, you can get straight at your work; you will be able to plunge deep into it, to get absorbed and to make progress; your attention will not be distracted, your effort scattered. Avoid half-work more than anything. Do not imitate those people who sit long at their desks but let their minds wander. It is better to shorten the time and use it intensely, to increase its value, which is all that counts.

Do something, or do nothing at all. Do ardently whatever you decide to do; do it with your might; and let the whole of your activity be a series of vigorous fresh starts. Half-work, which is half-rest, is good neither for rest nor for work.

Then invite inspiration. If the goddess does not always obey, she is always sensible of sincere effort. You must not strain yourself to excess, but you must find your direction, aim at your goal, and put out of your field of vision, like the marksman, everything else but the target. Renew the "spirit of prayer"; keep yourself in the state of eternity, your heart submissive to truth, your mind obeying its great laws, your imagination outspread like a wing, your whole being conscious of the silent stars above you, even by day, when they still shine faithfully. Beneath your feet, far below, will the sounds of life be; you will not notice them, you will hear only the music of the spheres which symbolizes in Scipio's Dream the harmony of the forces of creation.

Thus to open up one's being to truth, to withdraw from all else, and, if I may say so, to take a ticket for a different world, is true work. That is the kind of work of which we speak when we say that two hours daily are enough to yield a tangible worthwhile result. Evidently, they are not much; but they really suffice if all the conditions are fulfilled; and they are better than the fifteen hours a day that so many loud talkers boast of to the echoes.

Those fabulous figures have indeed been reached by certain people of abnormal capacity for work; they are instances of what might be called a lucky monstrosity, unless indeed that procedure be ruinous folly. Normal workers estimate at from two to six hours the time that can be steadily used with fruitful results. The principal question does not lie in the number of hours; but in their use and in the mind.

He who knows the value of time always has enough; not being able to lengthen it, he intensifies its value; and first of all he does nothing to shorten it. Time, like gold, has thickness; a solid medal, well struck and pure in line, has more value than the thin leaf from the gold-beater's hammer. Gold-beater, battage; the resemblance of the words is suggestive.[1] Many people are the dupe of appearances, of vague and muddle-headed intentions, talk all the time and never work.

We must remark that the period of intensive work cannot be any more uniform than our intellectual life as a whole. Proportionally, it has the same phases; one gets into swing gradually, sometimes with great difficulty, one reaches one's maximum, and then grows tired. There is a complete cycle: fresh morning, burning midday, evening de-

[1] *Battage,* a colloquial word for log-rolling, self-advertisement. The idea might be suggested in English by pairing the words gold-*beater,* drum-*beating.* (Tr. Note.)

cline. We must be the Josue of that evening, so that the battle which is always too short may be continued.

We shall have to speak later of the conditions of this careful economy of the work-time light; here I indicate only one: you must defend your solitude with a fierceness that makes no distinctions whatever. If you have duties, satisfy their demands at the normal time; if you have friends, arrange suitable meetings; if unwanted visitors come to disturb you, graciously shut the door on them.

It is important, during the hours sacred to work, not only that you should not be disturbed, but that you should know you will not be disturbed; let perfect security on that score protect you, so that you can apply yourself intensely and fruitfully. You cannot take too many precautions about this. Keep a Cerberus at your door. Every demand on you from outside is a loss of inner power and may cost your mind some precious discovery: "when half-gods go, the gods arrive." [1]

But note that this complete solitude, the only favorable atmosphere for work, need not be understood physically. Someone else's presence may double, instead of disturbing, your quietude. To have near you another worker equally ardent, a friend absorbed in some kindred thought or occupation, a chosen spirit who understands your work, joins in it, seconds your effort by silent affection and a keenness fired by your own—that is not a distraction, it is a help.

[1] Ralph Waldo Emerson. *Poems.*

Sometimes in the public libraries you breathe in a sense of concentration; it is like an atmosphere bearing you up. You are invaded by a sort of religious impression; you dare not fall short of it, or let your mind wander. The more you are surrounded by these adorers of the True in spirit and in truth, the more you are alone with the True alone, and the easier and more delightful your contemplation becomes.

A young couple in the husband's study, where the wife's work-table or basket has its place, where love reigns in silence, its wings outstretched to the wind of inspiration and some noble dream, is another picture of work. In the oneness of the life entered on by Christian marriage, there is a place for oneness of thought and the stillness necessary for it. The more two sister souls are together, the more secure they are against the outside world.

Yet the fact remains that solitude, once understood and arranged for, must be obstinately defended. You must listen to no one, neither indiscreet friends, nor ununderstanding relatives, nor chance comers, nor charity itself. You cannot be charitable in every direction at once. You belong to truth; serve her first. Except in certain clear and obvious cases, nothing should take precedence of your vocation.

The time of a thinker, when he really uses it, is in reality charity to all; only thus do we appreciate it properly. The man of truth belongs to the human race with truth itself; there is no risk of selfishness when one has isolated oneself jealously to serve this sublime and universal benefactor of mankind.

However, you must use your ingenuity to win the affectionate forgiveness of those from whom you turn away to work, and whom sometimes you hurt by doing so. Purchase your solitude; pay for your liberty by attentive thoughtfulness and kind acts of service. It is desirable that your retirement should be more advantageous to others than your companionship. In any case, let it be the least possible burden to them. Do your part, and let your relative independence be counterpoised by your absolute dependence when the time for your duties comes again.

chapter 5

The Field of Work

I. *Comparative Study*
II. *Thomism, the Ideal Framework for Knowledge*
III. *Our Specialty*
IV. *Necessary Sacrifices*

I

It is not possible to give any very exact advice as to what should be studied, and still less as to the proportion of the different elements to be included in a plan of work. St. Thomas makes no mention of these things in his *Sixteen Precepts*. In reality, this is a matter of personal vocation, closely dependent on the object in view. However, certain indications are possible, and they may afford a starting-point for profitable reflections.

We are not taking this question at its first beginnings; we are addressing people who have left schooldays behind and now propose to plan out or to complete deeper studies. At this level, the subject gives rise to P. Gratry's interesting observations on *Comparative Study*. It may appear that the development of this theme in *Les Sources* is somewhat out of date; but the substance remains and would deserve to be seriously considered by young intellectuals.

Comparative study: by that we mean widening our special work through bringing it into touch with all kindred disciplines, and then linking these specialties and the whole group of them to general philosophy and theology.

It is not wise, it is not fruitful, even if one has a very clearly limited special subject, to shut oneself up in it forthwith. That is putting on blinkers. No branch of knowledge is self-sufficing; no discipline looked at by itself alone gives light enough for its own paths. In isolation it grows narrow, shrinks, wilts, goes astray at the first opportunity.

A partial culture is always meager and precarious. The mind is all the time sensible of its deficiency; its workings are paralyzed by the lack of a certain freedom of movement, a certain sureness of outlook. A "dry fruit" stands for one who knows nothing; but also for one whose mind is shrunken and shrivelled because he has prematurely confined himself to the cultivation of one department of study.

We may assert without any paradox that every branch of science pursued home would lead to the other sciences, science to poetry, poetry and science to ethics, and then to politics and even to religion on its human side.

Everything is in everything, and partitions are only possible by abstraction. To abstract is not to lie, says the proverb: *abstrahere non est mentiri;* but that is on condition that the process of abstraction which distinguishes, methodically isolates, concentrates its light on a point, does not separate from its immediate object of study other things more or less directly belonging to it. To cut an object away from its connections is to present it falsely, for its links are part of itself.

Can one study a piece of clockwork without thinking of the adjoining piece? Can one study a bodily organ without considering the body? Neither is it possible to advance in physics or in chemistry without mathematics, in astronomy without mechanics and geology, in ethics without psychology, in psychology without the natural sciences, in anything without history. Everything is linked together, light falls from one subject on another, and an intelligent treatise on any of the sciences alludes more or less to all the others.

Therefore, if you want to have a mind that is open, clear, really strong, mistrust your specialty in the beginning. Lay your foundations according to the height that you aim to reach; broaden the opening of the excavation according to the depth it has to reach. But still you must understand that knowledge is neither a tower nor a well, but a human habitation. A specialist, if he is not a man, is a mere quill-driver; his egregious ignorance makes him like a lost wanderer among men; he is unadapted, abnormal, a fool. The intellectual Catholic will not copy such a model. Destined to serve the human race by his vocation, he wants first to belong to it as a man; he must walk boldly on the ground in stable equilibrium, not skipping on tiptoe.

In the pursuit of knowledge we have tried in

every direction to plumb the abyss of night; our learned men stretch out their hands to bring down the stars; the noble endeavor leaves no true thinker indifferent. To follow up to a certain point the explorations of every seeker is for you an obligation which results at last in a tenfold capacity for your own research. When you come back to your special study after having thus made a survey of different fields, widened your outlook, and acquired the sense of deep underlying connections, you will be quite a different man from the prisoner of one single narrow discipline.

Any branch of knowledge, cultivated by itself, not only does not suffice for itself, but presents dangers that all men of sense have recognized. Mathematics by themselves warp the judgment, accustoming it to a rigor that no other science admits of, still less real life. Physics, chemistry, obsess you by their complexity and give no breadth to the mind. Physiology leads to materialism; astronomy to vague speculation; geology turns you into a nosing hound; literature makes you hollow; philosophy inflates you; theology hands you over to false sublimity and magisterial pride. You must pass from one spirit to the other so as to correct one by the other; you must cross your crops in order not to ruin the soil.

And do not imagine that to carry this comparative study *to a certain point* is to overload yourself and to lose time about embarking on a special study. You will not overload yourself, for the lights thrown by one subject on another will, on the contrary, make everything easier; as you acquire breadth your mind will grow more receptive and less easily burdened.

By approaching the center of all ideas, everything is simplified, and what better means is there of approaching the center than to try different paths which all, like the radii of a circle, make us feel that we are converging on a common meeting-place?

I know a linguist who can make his way about a new language in a fortnight. Why?—Because he knows many others. At a glance he grasps the spirit of the new idiom, its fundamental characteristics, its whole structure. Now the different branches of knowledge are the different languages in which nature, the inexpressible, is laboriously stammered out by men; to decipher several of these languages helps each of them, for at bottom they are one.

Moreover, the vigorous instinct and the enthusiasm aroused in every man of good ability who moves about thus in the realms of knowledge, who explores those splendid territories as he might visit turn by turn the fiords of Norway, the Golden Horn, the burial chambers of Egypt, the prairies of America, and the palaces of China—that species of epic ardor which fires a strong intelligence in contact with the wonders of the mind, gives a marvelous zest and facility to study.

A rabbi, reproached with adding to the burdens of the law, answered: When a bushel is full of nuts, one can still pour into it many measures of oil. That man had zeal, which in regard of spiritual capacity corresponds to the heat which dilates bodies. A goblet in the sun has a greater capacity than in the shade. A mind in love with the spectacle of truth, outspread and shining with its light like the rainbow spanning heaven, grows capable of taking in without fatigue and with delight knowledge that would weary the man drearily confined to a single specialty.

Very great men have always shown themselves to be more or less universal: excelling in one branch, they were intelligently interested, often competent, sometimes specialized, in others. You could not have confined to a single department men like Aristotle, Bacon, Leonardo da Vinci, Leibnitz, or Goethe. Henri Poincaré used to astonish his colleagues of every section at the Academy of Science by his original views: to consult him was to put oneself at the center of knowledge, where the sciences cease to exist separately.

You do not aspire to anything like that? No: but proportionately to each one of us what the great have done remains an indication of what may be achieved. Make yourself a broad plan, which will gradually be narrowed down as regards the time devoted to each secondary study, but never as regards breadth of view and the spirit of your work.

Choose your advisers well. One among a thousand for the whole of your work, others for each part of it if necessary. Divide your time, regulate the order of your subjects: these things cannot be done at haphazard.

In everything go straight to what is essential; do

not linger over trifling points: it is not in small points that sciences are interconnected. It is often by detail, but by characteristic detail you get back again to the substance.

However, you cannot find your way in all these questions until you have taken in what we have yet to say.

Just as no particular branch of knowledge is self-sufficing so all branches together are not self-sufficing without the queen of knowledge, philosophy,[1] nor the whole of human knowledge without the wisdom springing from the divine science itself, theology.

Père Gratry expressed some capital truths on this point, and St. Thomas, still more profoundly, marked out the place and rank of these two queens of the double kingdom.[2] The sciences, without philosophy, discrown themselves and lose their direction. The sciences and philosophy without theology discrown themselves more lamentably, since the crown they repudiate is a heavenly one;

[1] It is remarkable that at the present time, the scientist is called on by his very science to elucidate problems that hitherto were of the exclusive domain of philosophy; causality, determinism, probability, continuity and discontinuity, space, time, etc. Logically, the scientist should borrow his notions from the philosopher; but most often the philosopher, satisfied with his age-old categories, declines the task of enlightening the scientist; and the scientist has to philosophize for himself, which he does without experience and often wrongly.

[2] See especially in the *Summa,* the whole of the *First Question;* in the Commentary on the *De Trinitate* of Boethius *Question II,* art. 2; in the *Contra Gentes,* Chapter I of the First Book.

and they go more irremediably astray, for earth without heaven cannot find the path of its orbit, nor the influences that give it fruitfulness.

Now that philosophy has failed in its duty, the sciences fall to a lower level and scatter their effort; now that theology is unknown, philosophy is sterile, comes to no conclusion, has no standard of criticism, no bearings for its study of history; it is often party-spirited and destructive, it is sometimes comprehensive and eclectic; it is never reassuring or really enlightening; it does not teach. And in the eyes of its masters who have the double misfortune to be ignorant and ignorant that they are ignorant, theology is a thing of the other world.

Yes, certainly, theology is of the other world in its object; but the other world bears up this world, continues it in every direction, backwards, forwards, upwards; and it is not surprising that it sheds light on it.

If the intellectual Catholic belongs to his time, he can do nothing better than work, for his part, at restoring the order that we lack. What, from the point of view of doctrine, is wanting in the knowledge of our time, is not positive content, it is harmony, a harmony that can come only from an appeal to first principles.[1]

The order of the mind must correspond to the order of things; and since the mind does not really

[1] Charles Dunan wrote this striking sentence: "For modern philosophy, transcendental problems are non-existent. But the converse is true: if these problems exist, it is modern philosophy that is non-existent." *Les Deux Idéalismes,* page 182, Paris, Alcan, 1911.

learn except by seeking out the relation of cause and effect, the order of the mind must correspond to the order of causes. If then there is a first Being and a first Cause, it is there that ultimate knowledge and light are attained. First as a philosopher, by means of reason, then as a theologian, utilizing the light from on high, the man of truth must center his research in what is at once the point of departure, the rule, the supreme and ultimate goal; in what is all to all things, and to all men.

Order among objects or disciplines of any kind is only established when principles, ranged in hierarchical importance up to the first principle, play their part as principles, as heads—as in an army, a well-ordered house, or a nation. Nowadays we have repudiated first principles, and knowledge is in a rout. We have mere fragments of nature's lore, shining tinsel ornaments and no garments, splendid chapters and no finished book, no Bible.

The Summae of old were the Bibles of knowledge: we have now no Summae, and no one among us is capable of writing one. Everything is in chaos. But at least, if a collective Summa is premature, every man who thinks and really desires to *know* can try to establish his personal Summa, that is to introduce order into his knowledge by an appeal to the principles of order; in a word, by philosophizing, and by crowning his philosophy with a concise but profound theology.

Christian scholars and scientists from the beginning of our era until the end of the seventeenth century, were all theologians; and men of learning whether Christians or not were all philosophers until the nineteenth century. Since then, knowledge has fallen to a lower level. It has gained in surface and lost in elevation, consequently also in depth, for the third dimension extends in two directions which correspond to each other. The Catholic, conscious of this aberration and of its consequences, must not fall a victim to it; if he is or desires to be an intellectual he must aim at complete intellectuality; he must attain all his dimensions.

Theology, said Père Gratry, has inserted a divine graft into the tree of knowledge, thanks to which this tree can bear fruits that are not its own. It loses nothing of its sap thereby, on the contrary, the sap circulates gloriously. As a result of this new and soaring impulse given to knowledge, of this appeal of the findings of human effort to the collaboration of heaven, all branches of knowledge are vivified and all disciplines broadened. The unity of faith gives to intellectual work the stamp of a vast cooperation. It is the collective operation of men united in God. And that is why Christian knowledge, as it now is, and still more as it will be when the Summa of modern times is written, cannot but exceed in fulness and in inspiration all the great works achieved by antiquity and by neo-paganism. The Encyclopedias [1] no more come near it than Babel does to our cathedrals.

It ought to be impossible for one who seeks truth

[1] An allusion to the *Encyclopédie,* the great monument of French free thought in the eighteenth century. (Tr. Note.)

to remain in ignorance of such a treasure. I hope that the coming generation, put on the track by the present one which is so manifestly in advance of its predecessors, will address itself seriously and without human respect to the science of sciences, the canticle of canticles of knowledge—to theology, the fount of inspiration and the only foundation of conclusive certainty. In it will be found both ripe thought and aspiration, the mighty, peaceful and transcendent joy which is the complete life of the mind.

It is not so difficult as people think to grasp the science of theology, nor is it a very long study to reach the degree of acquaintance with it that we have in view. It would be a different matter to take it up as a specialty. If you devote four hours a week to it for the five or six years needed to form the mind, that will be quite enough; afterwards you will only have to keep up what you know.

But beware above everything else of trusting false teachers. Go straight to St. Thomas of Aquin. Study the *Summa*, having first made sure to inform yourself exactly of the content of the faith. Have at hand the *Catechism of the Council of Trent*, which is in itself a masterly epitome of theology.[1] Get a good grip of that manual and continue day by day with St. Thomas the rational development of the divine science. The text will at first appear

[1] As a help, I venture to indicate the *Catéchisme des Incroyants*, published (by Flammarion) in order to make it easier for our contemporaries to understand Christian doctrine and its foundations.

dry, abstruse; then little by little the guiding lights will shine out; the first difficulties you overcome will be rewarded by fresh victories; you will learn the language of the country, and after some time you will move about in it as if you were at home—feeling indeed that it is your home and a glorious dwelling-place.

Study, of course, in Latin. Translations of the *Summa* often prove false to its thought; they are always inadequate. A man who would allow himself to be deterred by the slight effort needed to make his way about a language that an ordinary mind can master in two months would not deserve to have interest wasted on his mental training.[1] We are speaking to earnest students: let them, desiring to get into the "wine-cellar," take the trouble to find its key.

Some introductory book giving a preliminary idea and a first taste of the content of St. Thomas would be useful. Do not linger over it; but take the hand offered to give you a start.[2]

1 Some people, on reading this sentence, imagined that the author possessed a secret for teaching Latin in two months! He was not speaking of Latin, but of St. Thomas' language, which is to classical Latin pretty much what the Montagne Ste-Geneviève is to the Pic du Midi (the Montagne Ste-Geneviève is the rising ground on the south bank of the Seine, the old Paris University District [Tr. Note]). The Thomistic vocabulary is so limited, the turns of speech so often recur and are so free from the features that make Latin difficult, that really only laziness can hesitate when a treasure is to be had at the price of so slight an effort.

2 Cf. as an elementary work: Jacques Maritain, *Eléments de Philosophie,* Téqui 1920. For the more advanced student,

In another way, an open-minded and well-informed tutor would be an immense help in the beginning. I almost said an indispensable help. He would initiate you gradually into the special vocabulary of Thomism, would save you doubts and misunderstandings, would illustrate one text by another, would put you often on the right track and keep you from going astray. However, convinced as I am of the harm that can be done by unskillful friends, of the chilling effect and the sort of scandal caused by stupid commentaries, I advise you rather to work alone than with defective help. Try to crack the nut yourself; it will hurt your hands, but it will break, and St. Thomas himself will instruct his pupil.

For this end, as you read each article, consult carefully the different passages to which the editions refer you; consult the *Index Tertius*, an imperfect treasure, but a treasure all the same; compare text with text; make the different sources of information complete and illustrate one another, and draw up your own article. It is an excellent gymnastic, which will give your mind flexibility, vigor, precision, breadth, hatred of sophistry and of inexactitude, and at the same time insure you a progressively increasing store of notions that will be clear, deep, consecutive, always linked up with their first principles and forming by their interadaptation a sound synthesis.

A. D. Sertillanges, *Saint Thomas d'Aquin*, in the Collection des Grands Philosophes, Alcan 1910.

II

That leads me naturally to set out my idea of Thomism as the framework of comparative study.

It is undeniably useful to possess as early as possible, even at starting if it may be, a body of directive ideas forming a whole and capable, like the magnet, of attracting and subordinating to itself all our knowledge. The man without some such equipment is, in the intellectual universe, like the traveller who easily falls into skepticism through getting to know many dissimilar civilizations and contradictory doctrines.

This lack of a coherent system of ideas is one of the great misfortunes of our age. To escape it, thanks to the intellectual balance afforded by a sure body of doctrine, is an incomparable benefit. Now, in this respect Thomism is sovereign.

Here I expect protests. I had them in 1920,[1] I must foresee fresh ones. And so I think it well to say to anyone who is willing to put some trust in me: the longer I go on, the more convinced I am that the future of our intelligent Catholics really lies here—for their own intrinsic worth, and what is more and *more than anything,* for their adaptation to the present time. The partisans of the latest novelty may say what they like, the weight of a doctrine and its newness are two different things. Genius has no date. When eternal things are in question, it is wisdom to turn to the man who, at

[1] A reference to the earlier edition. (Tr. Note.)

any date in time, succeeded in piercing most deeply into the heart of eternity.

However, I must point out a danger here. Some people, dazzled by the glory of St. Thomas, open him enthusiastically. They are full of expectation. And having read two or three pages, they are disenchanted. The fact is that, unconsciously, they expected to find modish trinkets instead of heavy gold ingots, and very naturally are disappointed. But it is a mistake, in approaching the masterpieces of thought, or those of art or nature, to compare them with some vague and falsely magnificent preconceived idea. They cannot fit into such a framework. On the other hand, their solid perfections do exist, and it is stupid to miss them through not expecting them, or not adapting oneself to them.

I persist therefore in saying to the young Catholics who read me: study St. Thomas, he is the man of our day. You would think he had been created seven centuries ago to quench our thirst. Compared to the muddy water now served up to us, he is a clear spring. When by a vigorous effort you have overcome the first difficulties of an archaic mode of exposition, he reassures your mind, floods it with light, and provides a setting both strong and flexible for its further acquisitions.

Thomism is a synthesis. That does not mean that it is a complete system of knowledge; but a complete system of knowledge can find in it an almost miraculous power to coordinate and uplift. If a pope could say of St. Thomas' work in detail *Quot articula, tot miracula,* there is much more reason to say that the whole is something prodigious.

Study this system, appreciate its characteristics, assess the value of its leading ideas, then their order, the width of angle or better the vital capacity of every notion in regard of the facts and accessory notions that can enrich it: you will be astonished to see that no partial conspectus can compare with it for its force of attraction in respect of the whole of reality, that no seed has more power to absorb and canalize the juices of the earth.

The intellectual position of Thomism is so well chosen, so removed from all the extremes where abysses of error yawn, so central as regards the heights, that one is logically led up to it from every point of knowledge, and from it one radiates, along continuous paths, in every direction of thought and experience.

Other systems are opposed to adjacent systems: Thomism reconciles them in a higher light, taking account of what led them into error and careful to be just to all that is right in them. Other systems have been contradicted by facts: Thomism goes to meet facts, envelopes them, interprets them, classifies them, and establishes them as it were by legal right.

No metaphysic offers natural science more helpful principles of order and of higher interpretation; no rational psychology is in closer correspondence with all the discoveries of experimental psychology and its dependent sciences; no cosmology is more adaptable or readier to welcome the discoveries that have overthrown so many ancient fancies; no ethic is more favorable to the progress of the human conscience and human institutions.

I cannot attempt here even the slightest proof of the truth of these assertions; until each one experiences it for himself, he must accept it on trust. But must not the trust of the Catholic naturally go out to Her who has received the mission and the grace to guide from above the aspiration of his mind?

The Church believes today, as she believed from the first, that Thomism is an ark of salvation, capable of keeping minds afloat in the deluge of doctrine. She does not confuse it with faith, nor yet with knowledge in all its fulness; she knows that it is fallible, and that in respect of passing theories, it has shared the errors of different times; but she judges that its structure as a whole corresponds to the constitution of reality and of the intelligence, and she notes that both knowledge and faith converge on it, because it has taken up its position between them like a fortress at a meeting of the roads.

In such a domain one cannot lay down rules; but I say to the man who undertakes comparative study, that is, who resolves to carry on together as one single research special branches of study along with philosophy and theology: consult your powers; try to find in your heart enough faith in your age-old guide not to hesitate to give her willing and filial loyalty. If you can do that, your fidelity will have its reward; you will rise to a level unknown to proud self-reliance and to modernity with no eternal foundation.

III

We must immediately add something to what we have said about comparative study, lest someone should think that under this pretext we are urging anyone to try to acquire encyclopedic knowledge. Given certain conditions, the more one knows the better; but in fact, as these conditions cannot be realized, and today less than ever, the encyclopedic mind is an enemy of knowledge.

True knowledge, (*scientia,* science in its fundamental sense) lies in depth rather than in superficial extent. Science is knowledge through causes, and causes go down deep like roots. We must always sacrifice extent to penetration, for the reason that extent in itself is nothing, and that penetration, introducing us to the central point of observed facts, gives us the substance of what an interminable pursuit sought to discover.

We have pleaded for a certain extension, but it was for the sake of depth and as a means of mental formation; when this formation is attained and the possibilities of profound work are assured, we must begin to dig deep, and only specialization enables us to do this.

It oftens happens that what is indispensable at first becomes injurious later on. The harm would show itself here in many ways and would lead by different roads to mental deterioration.

In the first place, each individual has his capabilities, his resources, his interior or exterior difficulties, and each has to ask himself whether it would be wise to cultivate equally the things he is made for and those that are more or less beyond his grasp. To overcome a difficulty is good; it must be done; but intellectual life must not be an unbroken series of acrobatic feats. It is very important to work in joy, therefore with relative ease, therefore in the direction of one's aptitudes. By going forward at first on different paths each one must discover himself, and when he has found out his special vocation, pursue it.

Besides, a danger lies in wait for minds that spread themselves over too many subjects: the danger of being easily satisfied. Content with their voyages of discovery in every direction, they give up effort; their progress, rapid at first, is like that of the will o' the wisp on the ground. No energy continues to exert itself for long unless it is stimulated by increasing difficulty, and sustained by the increasing interest of some laborious investigation. When the whole field of study has been surveyed and its connections and unity estimated in the light of fundamental principles, it is urgently necessary, if one does not want merely to mark time, to turn to some task which is precise, defined in its limits, proportioned to one's strength; and then to throw oneself into it with all one's heart.

What we suggested a while ago has its converse here. We said that you must follow various paths awhile in order to get the sense of their meeting-points; you must try the ground in many directions in order to come at the deep places. Having done that, if you turn your whole attention to digging in the center, the apparent limitation is to the advantage of the whole space, the bottom of the hole reveals the whole sky. When one knows something thoroughly, provided one has some inkling of the rest, this rest in its full extent gains by the probing of the depths. All abysses resemble one another, and all foundations have communicating passages.

Moreover, supposing that one applies oneself with uniform and enduring energy to all branches of knowledge, one finds oneself speedily up against an impossible task. What will the result be? Wanting to be legion, one will have forgotten to be a person; trying to be a giant, one lessens one's stature as a man.

Everyone in life has his work; he must apply himself to it courageously and leave to others what Providence has reserved for others. We must keep from specialization as long as our aim is to become cultivated men, and, as far as concerns those to whom these pages are addressed, superior men; but we must specialize anew when we aim at being men with a function, and producing something useful. In other words, we must *understand* everything, but in order to succeed in *doing* some one thing.

IV

From that it follows that we are obliged at a given moment to accept necessary sacrifices. It is a painful thing to say to oneself: by choosing one road I am turning my back on a thousand others. Everything is interesting; everything might be useful; everything attracts and charms a noble mind; but death is before us; mind and matter make their demands; willy-nilly we must submit and rest content as to the things that time and wisdom deny us, with a glance of sympathy which is another act of homage to the truth.

Do not be ashamed not to know what you could only know at the cost of scattering your attention. Be humble about it, yes, for it shows our limitations; but to accept our limitations is a part of virtue and gives us a great dignity, that of the man who lives according to his law and plays his part. We are not much, but we are part of a whole and we have the honor of being a part. What we do not do, we do all the same; God does it, our brethren do it, and we are with them in the unity of love.

Therefore, do not imagine you can do everything. Measure yourself, measure your task; after some experiments, make up your mind, though without rigidity, to accept your limits; preserve, by reading and if necessary by a certain amount of writing, the advantage of your early studies, your contact with wide fields of knowledge—but for the main part of your time and strength, concentrate.

The half-informed man is not the man who knows only the half of things, but the man who only half knows things. Know what you have resolved to know; cast a glance at the rest. Leave to God, who will look after it, what does not belong to your proper vocation. Do not be a deserter from yourself, through wanting to substitute yourself for all others.

chapter 6

The Spirit of Work

I

Having determined the field of work, it is a good thing to note the spirit that should animate the worker; and we need first of all, before any special mode of its application, a spirit of earnestness. "Clear up your doubts" said St. Thomas to his disciple.

An active mind is constantly in search of some truth which for it, at the moment, is the representation of that integral truth to which it has vowed its service. The intelligence is like a child, whose lips never cease their *why*. Does a good educator leave this fruitful restless questioning unsatisfied? Does he not take advantage of this fresh curiosity, as of a youthful appetite, to give solid food to the nascent spiritual organism? Our soul does not age; it is always growing; in regard of truth it is always a child; we who have charge of its permanent education must not, as far as possible, leave any of the problems arising in the course of our work unsolved, or any of our investigations without an appropriate conclusion.

Let the man of study then be perpetually listening for truth. While he bends over his work, the Spirit breathes in him, reveals Himself perhaps from outside, sends His prophets—men, things, books, happenings; the attentive soul must neglect nothing of it all; for this spirit of truth, like grace, often passes by and does not come back. Is it not indeed itself a grace?

The great enemy of knowledge is our indolence; that native sloth which shrinks from effort, which does indeed consent now and then capriciously, to make a big effort but soon relapses into careless automatism, regarding a vigorous and sustained impetus as a regular martyrdom. A martyrdom, perhaps, given our make-up; but we must either be prepared for it or relinquish the idea of study: for what can be done without virile energy? "O God, Thou sellest all good things to men at the price of effort," wrote Leonardo da Vinci in his notes. He himself remembered it.

The mind is like the airplane which can only keep aloft by going forward with all the power of its propeller. To stop is to crash. On the other hand, earnestness and tenacity can carry us beyond all foreseen limits into regions undreamed of. People do not know how plastic the intelligence is and how capable of being trained to higher flights. Bossuet said: "The mind of man can make infinite discoveries, sloth alone puts limits to its wisdom and its inventions." What we take for a barrier is often but a thicket formed of our faults and our sensual negligences. Between conceiving and planning, planning and carrying out, carrying out and perfecting, how many delays there are, how many failures! The habit of effort brings these stages closer together, and carries the work from conception to completion along a rapid slope. The strong man rears the ladder of Jacob before him for the ascent and descent of the angels that visit us.

Some minds quickly reach the point of being satisfied with a given amount of knowledge. They work in the beginning, then lose the sense of the void always waiting to be filled. They do not remember that we are always void of what we have not, and that, in a limitless field of discovery, we never have reason to say: let us stop here. If we merely aim at display, or some advantage, a small stock of ideas may suffice. Many people get along like that with a sort of handy screen, concealing their vast ignorance from others and from themselves. But a real vocation is not so cheaply satisfied; it looks on every gain as a new starting-point. To know, to seek, to know more and to start afresh to seek more, is the life of a man devoted to truth, just as to make more money, whatever his fortune, is the aim of the miser. The intellectual who is sincere says every day to the God of truth: "The zeal of Thy house hath eaten me up."

As one grows older, one needs more than ever to be on one's guard against this temptation. We know the sort of people called "bonzes," learned old men panting beneath their honors, crushed with the demands made on them and wasting in public show the time they formerly devoted to making discoveries. Better equipped now, they have ceased to produce; supported in every way, they are nevertheless but the shadow of themselves. It was said of the painter Henner at the end of his life: "He only produces pseudo-Henners." I do not subscribe to that judgment, but it is a cruel saying, and to be feared by all who might lay themselves open to it. We must not blind ourselves to the fact that this premature dotage may be found even among the young who, pleased at a real or apparent happy hit, exploit it *ad nauseam* and waste on drawing out a finer and finer wire efforts that would be better spent casting an ingot or coining a medal.

A real thinker brings a very different spirit to his work; he is carried along by the instinct of a conqueror, by an urge, an enthusiasm, an inspiration, that are heroic. A hero does not stand still or set himself limits. A Guynemer looks on one victory as a rehearsal for another; with unfailing vigor he makes flight after flight, closes with an adversary, turns round on another, and only in death sees the end of his career.

We must always seek, always endeavor. Nature makes the wilderness flower anew, the star to shine, the water to flow down slopes, round obstacles, into empty places, dreaming of the sea that waits it yonder, and which it may at last reach. Creation in every one of its stages is continuous aspiration. The mind which is potentially all things can of itself no more limit its ideal forms than the natural forms of which they are a reflection. Death will set the limit, and so will our own inadequacy: let us at least have the courage to flee the frontiers marked out by laziness. Infinity, lying before us, demands infinity in our desire, to correct as far as may be the gradual failure of our powers.

II

The spirit of earnestness must go hand in hand with a habit of concentration that all men of deep thought recommend to us. Nothing is so disastrous as to keep turning one's attention this way and that. Light when diffused is lessened in geometrical progression. On the contrary, if you concentrate it through a lens, what it hardly warmed when it radiated freely takes fire at the focal point where the heat is intensified.

Let your mind become a lens, thanks to the converging rays of attention; let your soul be all intent on whatever it is that is established in your mind as a dominant, wholly absorbing idea. Make an orderly series of your different studies, so as to throw yourself into them completely. Let each task take entire hold of you, as if it were the only one. That was Napoleon's secret; it is the secret of all who are great in action. Men of genius themselves were great only by bringing all their powers to bear on the point on which they had decided to concentrate.

We must allow each thing its separate place, do

it in its own time, provide all the conditions necessary for the work, devote to it the fullest resources at our disposal, and once it has been brought to a successful issue, pass on quietly to something else. It is incredible what results one accumulates in that way without wearing oneself out in fussy agitation.

Not that one cannot have several undertakings in hand together: it is even necessary, for in order to stand back and get the right perspective, to arrive at a truer estimate of oneself and to correct oneself if need be, to rest from one effort by making another—and perhaps also for accidental motives—one cannot avoid interrupting one's tasks and substituting others. But then, what we say of concentration applies to each of these occupations and to every resumption of each of them. When the turn of one comes, we must put the other aside, set up a system of watertight compartments, work intensively at the point we are engaged on and not change to another until afterwards.

Doing a bit here and a bit there is never any good. The traveller who hesitates and tries different roads one after another, loses courage and makes no headway. On the contrary, to pursue one path steadily, to start off continually with fresh energy and then rest at the right moment—that is, when the first phase of activity is complete—is the way to produce our utmost, and at the same time to keep our mind fresh, our courage intact. The soul of a true worker, in spite of his preoccupations and the number of them that may press one on the other, should always, between two earnest endeavors to surmount some obstacle, remain as peaceful and noble as the cloud masses on the horizon.

We must add that this law of all activity applies more forcibly to the activity of pure thought, because of the unity of truth and the importance of keeping all its elements before our eyes, so that light may break on the mind. Every idea, provided it really is an idea, is infinitely rich; linked up with all others, it may revivify itself endlessly through them. As long as these enlightening interconnections go on revealing themselves, as long as truth emits its rays, do not turn your eyes aside, keep hold of the thread guiding you through the maze; sow the seed of a fertile thought, then again the seed of the new plant, do not weary of tilling or sowing; a single germ is good for a whole field.

All the productions of a well-endowed and well-formed mind should be nothing else than developments of a single thought, of a feeling for life seeking its forms and its applications. Did not M. Bergson recently tell us that again? "A philosopher worthy of the name," he writes, "never said more than one single thing." *A fortiori,* all the work of a particular period in connection with one subject or one spell of study, must be strictly disciplined in one direction. To dig and dig into the same hole is the way to get down deep and to surprise the secrets of earth.

One of the effects of this concentration is to bring about a selection in the confused mass of material that almost always confronts us at the beginning of our research. Gradually we shall discover the essential connections, and in that above all else consists the secret of great works. Worth is never in multiplicity, it lies in the relationships of a few elements which govern the whole subject under consideration or the whole essence of a person or thing; which reveal the underlying law and therefore enable us to produce an original creation, a work standing out in relief and of really important bearing. A few well-chosen facts, a few big ideas, big rather by their coherence and their interconnection than by their tenor, are matter enough for an inspired work. To direct their investigations well and to put their studies on a sound basis, was the whole art of the greatest men; we must try by their example to do the same, each of us, so as to use our powers to the fullest.

III

But there is something else still more important, namely, to submit not only to the discipline of work, but to the discipline of truth. This submission to truth is the binding condition for communion with it. Prompt obedience is what invites it to visit us. To this sacred meeting we must bring a respectful soul. Truth will not give itself to us unless we are first rid of self and resolved that it shall suffice us. The intelligence which does not submit is in a state of skepticism, and the skeptic is ill-prepared for truth. Discovery is the result of sympathy; and sympathy is the gift of self.

By thought we *find* things, we do not make

them; refusal to submit means missing them; not to meet them in a docile spirit is to evade the meeting. Yielding ourselves up to truth, and formulating it for ourselves as best we can but without any criminal infidelity, we perform an act of worship to which the God within us and the universal God will respond by revealing Their oneness and by communing with our soul. In that, as in everything, self-will is the enemy of God. This submission implies humility, and we should recall here what we said of the place of the virtues in the realm of intelligence; for all virtues are based on the exclusion of the proud personality, which resents order. Intellectually, pride is the father of aberrations and of artificial and pretentious productions; humility is the eye which reads in the book of life and in the book of the universe.

Study might be defined by saying that it is God becoming conscious in us of His work. Like every action, intellection passes from God to God, as it were, through us. God is its first cause; He is its last end; on the way, our too assertive self can deflect the movement. Let us rather open our eyes wisely so that our inspiring Spirit may see *in us.*

Our intellect is, taking it all in all, a passive faculty; one is intellectually strong in proportion as one is receptive. Not that we have not to react to the stimulus; but the vital reaction about which we shall speak at length must not change the tenor of our acquisitions, it must only make them our own. Wide culture, filling the mind with ideas, starts it on new lines of thought and increases its capacity; but without humility this force of attraction exerted on the outside world will be a fresh source of falsehood. On the contrary, to a cultured and humble mind, flashes of light come from all sides, and strike on it as the rays of dawn do on the hilltops.

Besides humility, we must recommend to the thinker a certain passivity of attitude which corresponds to the nature of the mind and of inspiration. We do not know very well how the mind works; but we know that passivity is its first law. Still less do we know how inspiration comes; but we can notice that it utilizes our unconsciousness more than our initiative. We go forward amid difficulties like a rider in the night; it is better to trust our mount than to pull unwisely on the bridle.

Activity which is too intentional makes our intelligence less sure and less receptive; if we strive too anxiously, we remain shut up in ourselves, whereas to understand is to become *other,* and in happy receptivity to let truth pour in upon us. Try to project your thought into the object of knowledge, not to keep it within yourself; as in speaking one must speak out into space, not into one's sinuses. Singers know what I mean; those who have experienced inspiration will understand me also. You must look through the mind in the direction of things, not into the mind, which is more or less forgetful of things. In the mind we have the means of seeing, not the object of sight: let the means not distract us from the goal.

"The essential thing is to be in a state of ecstasy,"[1] writes the fresco painter Louis Dussour, "yet trying all the while to understand the connections and the structure of things." Sometimes the ecstasy is lacking, sometimes the constructive faculty. But here we are speaking of the first.

Profound work consists in this: to let the truth sink into one, to be quietly submerged by it, to lose oneself in it, not to think that one is thinking, nor that one exists, nor that anything in the world exists but truth itself. That is the blessed state of ecstasy.

For St. Thomas, ecstasy is the child of love; it carries you out of yourself, toward the object of your dreams. To love truth ardently enough to concentrate on it and so be transported into the universal, into what is, into the heart of abiding truths, is the attitude of contemplation and of fruitful production. One is then in a sense like the animal in the forest, concentrated, watchful, crouching with his eye on his prey; and the inner life is intense, but with a sense of distance as if one were moving among the stars. One feels at once delivered from all trammels and yet enchained, free and enslaved; one is fully oneself in surrendering to what is above self; one exults while forgetting self: it is a nirvana in which the intelligence is intensely happy and active.

Do not then discourage this spirit if it visits you, driving it away in favor of some artificial and external form of work. If it is absent, hasten its re-

[1] See pp. ix, 31, 255.

turn by your humble desires. In the divinely dazzling light, you have more to gain in a short time than in a long period given up to your own abstract thoughts. "Better is one day in thy courts, O Lord, above thousands." [1]

Avoid as long as possible the return of your deliberate activity, the awakening of the Spouse. Let your mind be the wax, not the seal; so that the stamp of truth may remain pure. Practice holy abandonment; obey God; be like the inspired poet, like the orator lifted on an inner wave for whom thought has ceased to be a burden.

On the other hand, having to learn from men by reading, teaching, contact, appreciate the sense of this golden rule inserted by St. Thomas in the middle of his *Sixteen Precepts:* "Do not consider from whom you hear things, but entrust to your memory everything good that is said."

The history of the sciences teems with examples of the resistance of talent to talent, genius to genius, coterie to coterie, clique to clique. Laënnec opposes Broussais, Pouchet opposes Pasteur; Lister has England against him, Harvey the whole of humanity above forty years of age. You would think that truth was too prolific and that its rapid multiplication had to be checked! And yet the laws of the world reign over matter; why has mind such difficulty in forcing the assent of mind?

In the First Epistle to the Corinthians, Chapter 14, we read that if to the least of the faithful is

[1] Ps. 83:11.

given a revelation in prayer, the others must be silent and listen. On this St. Thomas makes this reflection: "No one, however wise, should reject the teaching of another, however insignificant";[1] and that concords with another Pauline counsel: "Each of you must have the humility to think others better men than himself" (Phil. 2:3).[2] The superior man at any moment is he who is nearest to the truth and receiving its light.

What matters in an idea is not its origin but its magnitude; what is interesting in genius itself is not the person: neither Aristotle, nor Leibnitz, nor Bossuet, nor Pascal, but the truth. The more precious an idea is, the less it matters where it comes from. Train yourself to indifference about sources. Truth alone has a claim, and it has that claim wherever it appears. As we must not swear allegiance to anyone, so still less must we disdain anyone; and if it is not expedient to believe everybody neither must we refuse to believe anyone who can show his credentials.

That is our great liberty. This readiness to accept truth brings so rich a reward that it would tempt even avarice itself, if the avaricious thinker did not imagine it wiser to sit guarding his own coffers. We like to believe that we possess everything, that we are capable of everything, and we give but an inattentive hearing to the voice of others. We make a few favored exceptions, men or books; they have our ear and afford us inspiration.

1 *In Evang. Joann.* C.IX. lect. 3, end.
2 Msgr. Knox's translation.

Now in reality there is inspiration everywhere; the breath of the Spirit fills the valleys just as it blows upon the mountaintops. In the meanest intelligence is a reflection of infinite Wisdom, and deep humility is able to recognize it.

How is it possible not to feel oneself in the presence of God when a man is teaching? Is he not God's image? An image sometimes distorted, but often authentic; and the distortion is always partial. It would be more profitable to ask ourselves how the image may be rectified, and how far it remains true, than to shrug our shoulders or indulge in fierce opposition. Opposition is always useless; reflection is better. Wherever the God of truth has left something of Himself, we must eagerly welcome it, venerate it religiously and utilize it diligently. Where the eternal Sower has passed, shall we not gather in the harvest?

IV

Lastly, in order to ennoble the spirit of our work, we must add to earnestness, concentration, submission, an effort at breadth which will give to each study or to each product of our thought a kind of universal bearing.

A problem cannot be self-contained; by its very nature it exceeds its own limits; for the intelligibility that it presupposes is borrowed from sources higher than itself. What we have said of comparative study guides us here. Every object of our investigation belongs to a whole in which it acts and is acted upon, in which it is subject to conditions and imposes its own; one cannot study it apart. What we call specializing or analysis may indeed be a method, it must not be a spirit. Shall the worker be the dupe of his own device? I isolate a bit of mechanism so as to see it better; but while I hold it in my hand and examine it with my eyes, my thought must keep it in its place, see it move as part of a whole—otherwise I am falsifying the truth both as regards the whole mechanism which I have made incomplete, and as regards the part which has become incomprehensible.

The True is a single whole; all things are connected in the one supreme Truth; between a particular object and God all the laws of the world are operating, ever increasing in amplitude, from the norm governing that particular object up to the eternal Axiom. On the other hand, man's mind also is a unity; it cannot be satisfactorily formed on the false idea of specialties considered as a breaking-up of the true and the beautiful into scattered fragments. However restricted your investigation may be, however minute the subject that you are pursuing, the whole of man and the universe are really involved. The subject and the object both tend to the universal. Truly to study a thing means evoking step by step the sense of all other things and of their solidarity—mingling in the concert of all beings, entering into union with the universe and with oneself.

We spoke a moment ago of concentration; but it was clear that we did not thereby seek to narrow down our study. To concentrate and to look abroad are a systole and diastole, one and the same movement. I call concentration the convergence of the attention on a point; I call looking abroad the sense that this point is the center of a vast whole, indeed the center of everything, for in the infinite sphere "the center is everywhere and the circumference nowhere" (Pascal).

Our mind has this double tendency—to unify details so as to arrive at a comprehensive synthesis; and to lose the sense of unity by lingering too long with details. We must balance these two tendencies. The first corresponds to the aim of science, the second to our weakness. We must isolate things to penetrate them more deeply, but then we must unite them in order better to understand them.

Do not therefore, when you work, take too low a point of view. Think high. Keep the soul of a seer while plucking the little twigs of truth, and, what is still more obviously necessary, do not reduce sublime questions to petty proportions. Be conscious that you are touching on great secrets, sharing the inspiration of great souls; perceive the light that trickles in here or there, while farther off, in continuity with this slender gleam, it floods worlds as it flows unbrokenly from the pure Source of all things.

Corot does not paint a tree and forget the horizon; Velásquez poses his Meninas[1] in mid-Escurial, in mid-life, better still in mid-Being; for it is that feeling for the mystery of Being that turns

[1] *Las Meninas*, the Maids of Honour, a picture by Velásquez in the Museo del Rey, Madrid. (Tr. Note.)

his prodigious talent into genius, genius that holds the soul spellbound while it charms the eye. It is a rule of the art of painting to think principally of what is not included in the picture, to know that the fragment painted should yield in importance to the *character,* to the general bearing of the subject, to its broad development beyond the canvas.

The artist, apropos of the least detail, must be in a state of musing, the writer, the philosopher, the orator in a state of thinking and feeling, about the universe. As one puts a finger on a point of the globe, one must feel its full extent and its roundness. We are always speaking of the whole.

Flee those minds that can never rise above their academic rules, that are the slaves of their work instead of doing it in the fulness of light. It is a mark of inferiority plainly in contradiction with an intellectual vocation to allow oneself to be tied down by narrow prescriptions and to have one's mind benumbed into bookish forms. Helots or eternal children: such are those pretended workers who are out of their element in any higher region, in face of any broad horizon, and who would like to reduce others to their narrow elementary school orthodoxy.

It is the mark of genius to see, in one's work, what will not go into it; in books what they cannot express. The real treasure of a great book is what is between the lines; it suggests; it makes one reflect that nothing is foreign to the deepest thoughts of man. Therefore, instead of narrowing down restricted subjects and emptying them of all content, lend to them what gives them their solid worth—that is, lend them what does not belong to them alone, but is common to them and other subjects, indeed to all subjects as light is common to colors and to their distribution over objects.

The ideal would be to establish in one's mind a common life of thoughts all interconnected and forming, as it were, only one. So it is in God. Can there be a better model to guide from afar our humble knowledge?

The spirit of contemplation and of prayer that we have pleaded for would of itself bring us nearer to that state: it is its natural fruit. By taking God's point of view thanks to which everything finds its ultimate dependence, and all things their cohesion, one cannot but feel oneself at the center of things, solicited by inexhaustible riches and possibilities.

Anyone who takes the trouble to think will realize that the kind of dazzlement we feel at the vision of a new truth is linked with this sense of indefinite vistas and universal connections. This one single step in the direction of the true is like a sunlit excursion. One sees the world under a new light, one feels the whole universe vibrating in contact with the fragment discovered. Later on, this idea, reduced to its own dimensions after having played the part of a forerunner, may seem petty to him whom it dazzled; with no reverberation outside itself, it seems lifeless, it disappoints the feeling for the infinite which is the soul of all research.

Great men have suffered from this shrinkage of their thoughts. Their vision was great, they find the results petty. For that reason we must read them, even them, in an unliteral, un-bookish spirit, seeing beyond them with an understanding that will in reality restore them to their true self. The letter kills: let reading and study be spirit and life.

V

Enough has been said to show that the sense of mystery must remain, even after our maximum effort and even after truth has seemed to smile on us. Those who think that they understand everything prove by that alone that they have grasped nothing. Those who rest satisfied with provisional answers to problems that in reality remain unsolved, warp the answer given them, not knowing that it is partial. Every question is an enigma set us by nature and through nature by God: the questions God proposes, God alone can answer. The gates of the infinite are always open. The most precious part of anything is what is not expressed. Was it not Biot [1] who, addressed by a colleague in the words: "I am going to ask you an interesting question," replied: "It's no use: if your question is interesting, I do not know the answer." "We do not know all of anything" says Pascal; and Claude Bernard [2] adds: "To understand a single thing thoroughly, we should understand all things." One may say of the full truth in any subject whatever the same thing that St. Augustine said of God: "If you understand, say to yourself that your reasoning

[1] A French physicist and astronomer, 1774-1862. (Tr. Note.)
[2] A great French physiologist, 1813-1878. (Tr. Note.)

is astray." But the man of petty mind imagines that he possesses the cosmos and what it contains; carrying a pail in his hand with a gallon of shimmering water he says: "Look, I have got hold of the ocean and the stars."

St. Thomas at the end of his life, overcome by this sense of the mystery of the All, answered Brother Reginald who was urging him to write: "Reginald, I can no more: all that I have written seems to me but straw." Let us not have the presumption to wish that this lofty despair should come to us too soon: it is a reward; it is the silence preceding the great cry with which the whole soul will vibrate in the flood of light revealed; but a little of that awe is the best corrective for the pride that blinds and the pretensions that mislead us. Besides, it stimulates us to work, for distant lights attract us as long as we have the hope of reaching them. On the contrary, if we think that everything has been said and that we have only to learn, we work in a little circle and stick fast in the same spot.

A noble character knows that our lights are only the degrees of shadow by which we climb toward the inaccessible light. We stammer, and the enigma of the world remains unsolved. Study means specifying a few conditions, classifying a few facts; great and fruitful study comes only from putting the little we achieve under the favoring direction of what we do not yet know. That does not mean consigning it to darkness; for it is the light we do not see that best sustains the dim reflections of our astral night.

Mystery is in all things the light of what we know; just as unity is the source of number, and immobility the secret of the dizziest speed. To perceive in oneself the murmur of all being and all duration, to appeal to their witness, is, in spite of their silence, to assure oneself the best guarantees for the acquisition of truth. Everything is linked with everything, and the clearly visible relations of things have their roots in the night into which I am groping my way.

chapter 7

Preparation for Work

Reading

I

Work means learning and producing; in both cases a long preparation is needed. For production is a result; and in order to learn, when the subject matter is difficult or complex, one must first have gone through what is simple and easy: "You must go to the sea by the streams, and not all at once," St. Thomas tells us.

Now reading is the universal means of learning, and it is the proximate or remote preparation for every kind of production.

We never think entirely alone: we think in company, in a vast collaboration; we work with the workers of the past and of the present. The whole intellectual world can be compared, thanks to reading, to a great editorial or mercantile office, where each one finds in those about him the initiation, help, verification, information, encouragement, that he needs.

It is therefore a primordial necessity for the man of study to know how to read and to utilize his reading, and would to heaven that people were not habitually oblivious of the fact!

The first rule is to read little. In 1921, in *Le Temps,* Paul Souday,[1] having it appears some grudge to vent on me, caught on to this precept: "Read little," and tried to find in it an obscurantist spirit. My reader knows what that objection is worth. Paul Souday certainly knew it quite as well.

I am not advising anyone to limit his reading stupidly: all the foregoing chapters would give the lie to such an interpretation. We want to develop breadth of mind, to practice comparative study, to keep the horizon open before us; these things cannot be done without much reading. But *much* and *little* are opposites only in the same domain. Here much is necessary in the absolute sense, because the work to be done is vast; but little, relatively to the deluge of writing that, even in the most restricted special fields, floods our libraries and our minds nowadays.

What we are proscribing is the passion for reading, the uncontrolled habit, the poisoning of the mind by excess of mental food, the laziness in disguise which prefers easy familiarity with others' thought to personal effort.

The passion for reading which many pride them-

[1] A notable literary critic, of rationalistic and positivist turn of mind. (Tr. Note.)

selves on as a precious intellectual quality, is in reality a defect; it differs in no wise from the other passions that monopolize the soul, keep it in a state of disturbance, set up in it uncertain currents and cross-currents, and exhaust its powers.

We must read intelligently, not passionately. We must go to books as a housekeeper goes to market when she has settled her menus for the day according to the laws of hygiene and wise spending. The mind of the housekeeper at the market is not the mind she will have in the evening at the cinema. She is not now thinking of enjoyment and dazzled wonderment, but of running her house and seeing to its well-being.

The mind is dulled, not fed, by inordinate reading, it is made gradually incapable of reflection and concentration, and therefore of production; it grows inwardly extroverted, if one can so express oneself, becomes the slave of its mental images, of the ebb and flow of ideas on which it has eagerly fastened its attention. This uncontrolled delight is an escape from self; it ousts the intelligence from its function and allows it merely to follow point for point the thoughts of others, to be carried along in the stream of words, developments, chapters, volumes.

The continual sight stimuli thus occasioned destroy mental energy, as constant vibration wears out steel. There is no real work to be expected from the great reader, when he has overstrained his eyes and the membranes of his brain; he is in a state of chronic mental headache, while the wise worker, preserving his self-control, calm and clear-headed, reads only what he wants to retain, retains only what will be useful, manages his brain prudently and does not abuse it by cramming it absurdly.

Better go out of doors, read in the book of nature, breathe fresh air, relax. After the requisite activity, arrange for the requisite recreation, instead of automatically yielding to a habit which is intellectual only in its matter, which in itself is as commonplace as gliding down a slope or climbing hills aimlessly.

People talk of keeping *au courant,* and no doubt an intellectual cannot ignore the human race, nor be indifferent to what is written in his special field; but take care lest the current should carry away with it all your capacity for work, and, instead of bearing you onwards, prevent you from making any headway against it. It is only by rowing oneself that one goes forward; no current can take you to the point you aim at reaching. Go your own way and do not drift into the wake of everybody else.

What you must principally cut down is the less solid and serious kind of reading. There must be no question at all of poisoning your mind with novels. One from time to time, if you like, as a recreation and not to neglect some literary glory, but that is a concession; for the greater number of novels upset the mind without refreshing it; they disturb and confuse one's thoughts.

As to newspapers, defend yourself against them with the energy that the continuity and the indiscretion of their assault make indispensable. You must know what the papers contain, but they contain so little; and it would be easy to learn it all without settling down to interminable lazy sittings! Anyhow, there are hours more suitable than working hours for running after the news.

A serious worker should be content, one would think, with the weekly or bi-monthly chronicle in a review; and for the rest, with keeping his ears open, and turning to the daily papers only when a remarkable article or a grave event is brought to his notice.

I sum up what I want to say in this connection: never read when you can reflect; read only, except in moments of recreation, what concerns the purpose you are pursuing; and read little, so as not to eat up your interior silence.

II

The principle of choice is already included in these first remarks. "What discernment we should exercise," said Nicole, "about the things that feed our mind and are to be the seed of our thoughts! For what we read unconcernedly today will recur to our minds when occasion arises and will rouse in us, even without our notice, thoughts that will be a source of salvation or ruin. God stirs up the good thoughts to save us; the devil stirs up the evil thoughts of which he finds the seed in us." [1]

[1] Nicole, *Essais de morale contenus en divers traités,* V.II, Paris 1733, p. 244.

You must then choose—which means two things, to choose books and to choose in books.

Choose your books. Do not trust interested advertising and catchy titles. Have devoted and expert advisers. Go straight to the fountainhead to satisfy your thirst. Associate only with first-rate thinkers. What is not always possible in personal relations is easy, and we must take advantage of it, in our reading. Admire wholeheartedly what deserves it, but do not lavish your admiration. Turn away from badly written books, which are probably poor in thought also.

Read only those books in which leading ideas are expressed at first hand. These are not very numerous. Books repeat one another, water one another down, or contradict one another, and that too is a kind of repetition. On examination we find that discoveries in thought are rare. The old stock or rather the permanent stock of ideas is the best; one must take one's stand on it in order truly to commune with the intelligence of man, far from petty, stammering, squabbling individualities.

It was a milliner (Mlle. Bertin) who aptly said: "There is nothing new but what is forgotten." The majority of writers only edit and publish other writers' thoughts: that is something, but the original author himself appeals to me.

Therefore, you will read with an open mind anything good that is written; you will take account of what is of present interest; you will take still more account of actuality in matters of information, of positive notions that are evolving or growing; for you want to be a man of your time, not an archaic specimen. But on the other hand, have no superstitious respect for novelty; love the eternal books that express eternal truths.

Next you must choose in your books, where not everything is of equal value. Do not on that account assume the attitude of a judge; be to your author rather a brother in truth, a friend, and even a humble friend since, at least in certain respects, you are taking him for your guide. The book is your elder; you must pay it honor, approach it without pride, read it without prejudice, bear with its faults, seek the grain in the chaff. But you are a free man, you remain responsible; hold back sufficiently to keep possession of your own soul and if need be to defend it.

"Books are the works of men," to quote Nicole again, "and the corruption of man taints most of his actions, and as it consists in ignorance and concupiscence, almost all books have something of these two faults." [1] Therefore it is often necessary in the course of one's reading to filter what one reads so as to purify it. For that, we must trust God and our better self, the self which is the child of God and in which an instinct for truth, a love of the good, will serve as a safeguard. But remember besides that the value of a book is partly your own value, and what you are capable of getting out of it. Leibnitz made use of everything; St. Thomas took from the heretics and the paganizers of his day an enormous number of thoughts, and none of

[1] *Op. cit.* p. 246.

them did him any harm. An intelligent man finds intelligence everywhere, a fool projects on every wall the shadow of his narrow and inert brow. Do your best to choose; but try to secure that all shall be good, wide, attuned to truth, prudent, and progressive: because these qualities are your own.

III

To be a little more precise, I distinguish four kinds of reading. One reads for one's formation and to become somebody; one reads in view of a particular task; one reads to acquire a habit of work and the love of what is good; one reads for relaxation. There is *fundamental* reading, *accidental* reading, *stimulating* or *edifying* reading, *recreative* reading.

All these kinds of reading must be regulated as we have just said; each kind has also its particular requirements. Fundamental reading demands docility, accidental reading demands mental mastery, stimulating reading demands earnestness, recreative reading demands liberty.

When one's mind is in process of formation and one has almost everything to learn, the hour has not come for individual initiative. Whether one is at the earlier stage, acquiring all-round culture, or taking up a new branch of study, a problem hitherto neglected, the authors consulted for this purpose must be believed rather than criticized, and followed in their own line of thought rather than used according to the reader's views. To launch out into action too soon interferes with the process of acquisition; it is wise at first to be docile. "You must believe your master," says St. Thomas, repeating Aristotle. He himself did this and found it to his advantage.

It is by no means a question of blind obedience, a noble mind does not go in chains; but as the art of commanding is learned only by obedience, mastery of thought is obtained only through discipline. A provisional attitude of respect, confidence, faith, as long as one does not possess all the elements of judgment, is so evident a necessity that only the conceited and the presumptuous refuse to accept it.

No one is infallible, but the pupil is much less so than the master; and if he refuses to listen, for once that he is right he will miss the truth a dozen times and will fall a victim to appearances. On the contrary, to give credence to the master and to be relatively passive, conceding to him something of what is due to truth, is to the advantage of truth itself, and enables the pupil at last to utilize even the deficiencies and illusions of the teacher. One only knows what a man lacks by estimating his wealth.

It is elementary wisdom beforehand to choose among a thousand the guides whom one will thus trust. The choice of an intellectual father is always a serious thing. We have advised St. Thomas for the highest doctrines. One cannot confine oneself to him; but all that is necessary is to know thoroughly three or four authors for one's specialty, and about the same number for each problem that arises. One will have recourse to other books for *information,* not for *formation,* and the attitude of mind will no longer be the same.

It will even in certain respects be the inverse, for the person who seeks information, who wants to use it, is not in a state of pure receptivity; he has his own idea, his plan; the work consulted becomes his servant. A modicum of docility is always necessary; but now it is directed to truth rather than to the writer; and in as far as the writer is concerned, it gives him credence to the point perhaps of not disputing his conclusions, yet does not slavishly follow every step of his procedure.

These questions of attitude are extremely important; for to consult books in the same way as you study them is loss of time; and to study as if you were merely consulting them means remaining your own master and losing the benefits of formation offered you by one who could initiate you into his subject.

He who reads in view of a piece of work has his mind dominated by what he aims at doing; he does not dive into the water, he draws from it; he stands on the bank, preserves the freedom of his movements; he confirms his own idea at each borrowing instead of sinking it in the idea of another; and he lays down his book enriched, not dispossessed of what he brought to it—for that would happen if the fascination of the reading interfered with the purpose of utilizing it which was its justification.

With regard to stimulating reading, the choice,

apart from our general rules, must depend on each one's experience. What has already helped you may very likely help you again. An influence may in the long run wear itself out; but at first it acts more strongly every time, habit quickens it, a deeper penetration acclimatizes it in us; the association of ideas and feelings connects a given page with states of soul that it brings back.

It is an immense resource in movements of intellectual or spiritual depression to have in this way your favorite authors, your inspiriting pages; to keep them at hand, always ready to invigorate you. I know certain persons who for years whenever their spirits flagged got a fresh start from the peroration of the *Oraison funèbre* on the Great Condé.[1] Others, in the spiritual domain, are irresistibly moved by Pascal's *Mystère de Jésus,* by a *Prayer* of St. Thomas, by a chapter of the *Imitation* or by one of the parables. Each one should watch himself, note what helps him, keep at hand together his remedies for the sicknesses of the soul and not hesitate to go back and back to the same cordial or the same antidote until these have utterly lost their efficacy.

In the matter of reading for relaxation choice seems much less important. Relatively indeed it is so; but let no one imagine that it is all the same to find distraction in this or in that, when the object is to come back in the best of conditions to what is

[1] One of the most impressive of Bossuet's famous *Oraisons funèbres.* (Tr. Note.)

our *raison d'être*. Certain kinds of reading are not recreative enough; others are too much so, to the detriment of the recollection that must come afterwards; others again may divert [1] you, in the etymological sense, I mean, that is turn you aside from your path.

I know a man who rested from a laborious piece of work by reading Zeller's *History of Greek Philosophy:* it was a distraction, but not a sufficient one. Others read highly spiced or fantastic stories which provide a complete change of mental scene; for others their light reading is an indulgence in temptations which discourage them from work and harm their soul. All that is bad. If books are your servants like other objects that you use in daily life, those in particular that play only an accessory part must be made to serve. Do not sacrifice yourself to your fan.

Many thinkers have found habitual relief and attraction in stories of travel and exploration, in poetry, art criticism, reading of plays, memoirs. Each one has his tastes, and taste in this matter is the capital thing. One thing alone according to St. Thomas gives real rest: joy; to seek distraction in something boring would be a delusion.

Read something that you like, that does not excite you too much, that does not harm you in any way; and since even when you seek distraction you are leading the consecrated life, have the intelligence to read, among the books that are equally

[1] In the French, *dévoyer,* literally turn from the path, turn astray. (Tr. Note.)

effective in resting your mind, what will also be useful otherwise, helping you to develop your personality, to adorn your mind, to be a man.

IV

I want to dwell especially, for I attach extreme importance to it in the conduct of the mind and of life, on the use to be made of great men. Contact with genius is one of the choice graces that God grants to humble thinkers; we should prepare for it as according to the Scripture we should prepare for prayer, as we pull ourselves together and assume an attitude of respect when we are to meet a great personage or a saint.

We think too little of the privilege of this bond with the greatest minds. It multiplies the joy and profit of living, it enlarges the world and makes it a nobler and more precious place to live in, it renews for each man the glory of being a man, of having his mind open on the same horizons as the greatest, of living on high levels and of forming with his fellows, with those who afford him inspiration, a society in God. "Next after men of genius come those who can recognize their worth," said Thérèse Brunswick, speaking of Beethoven.

To recall from time to time the names of those who shine with special brilliance in the firmament of the intelligence is to dip into the record of our titles to nobility; and this pride has the same beauty and efficacy as the pride that a son takes in an illustrious father or a great ancestry.

If you are a man of letters, do you not appreciate the advantage of having behind you Homer, Sophocles, Virgil, Dante, Shakespeare, Corneille, Racine, La Fontaine, Pascal? If you are a philosopher, would you be without Socrates, Plato, Aristotle, St. Thomas of Aquin, Descartes, Leibnitz, Kant, Maine de Biran, Bergson? As a scientist, do you realize all that you owe to Archimedes, Euclid, Aristotle again, Galileo, Kepler, Lavoisier, Darwin, Claude Bernard, Pasteur? As a religious man think how much poorer all souls would be if they had not, along with St. Paul, saints Augustine, Bernard, Bonaventure, the author of the Imitation; St. Catherine of Siena, St. Teresa, Bossuet, St. Francis of Sales, Newman.

The communion of saints is the support of the mystical life; the banquet of the sages, perpetuated by our assiduous cult, is the invigoration of our intellectual life. To cultivate the faculty of admiration and because of it to keep constantly in familiar touch with illustrious thinkers, is the means, not of equalling those whom we honor, but of equalling our own best self; and that, I repeat, is the objective to be visualized and pursued.

Contact with writers of genius procures us the immediate advantage of lifting us to a higher plane; by their superiority alone they confer a benefit on us even before teaching us anything. They set the tone for us; they accustom us to the air of the mountaintops. We were moving in a lower region; they bring us at one stroke into their own atmosphere. In that world of lofty thought, the face of truth seems to be unveiled; beauty shines forth; the fact that we follow and understand these seers makes us reflect that we are after all of the same race, that the universal Soul is in us, the Soul of souls, the Spirit to whom we have only to adapt ourselves in order to burst into divine speech, since at the source of all inspiration, always prophetic, there is "God, the first and supreme author of all one writes." [1]

When a man of genius speaks, we are inclined to think him quite simple; he expresses humanity, and an echo within us responds to him. When he relapses into silence, can we not continue in the same mode and terminate the unfinished period? Alas, no! As soon as he leaves us to ourselves, we return to our previous powerlessness, we stammer: yet we know that the true expression exists, and our stammerings begin to have a different tone.

Listen to certain Preludes of Bach. They do not say much; there is a short motif repeated; then insistent variations in no higher relief than that of a medal by Roty.[2] But what a level of inspiration! Into what an unknown world we are transported! To stay there and move freely in it would be our dream. We can at least go back there in memory, and what a blessing it is to be able to rise so far above futilities! It refines us, and helps us to pass a just judgment on the brilliant but foolish display of fireworks that often forms the staple of intellectual entertainments.

[1] Victor Hugo.

[2] An illustrious French sculptor and engraver, 1846-1911. (Tr. Note.)

Again, when genius supplies us with themes, reveals truths to us, opens up regions of mystery and sometimes, like a Thomas of Aquin or a Goethe, presents us with centuries of culture concentrated in a single person, what a debt we are under! "The human mind cannot go very far," wrote Rodin, "except on this condition: that the thought of the individual be added patiently and silently to the thought of the generations." The great thinker then who in his own person sums up for us the thought of generations enables us to go far with his help; he gives us a claim to the domains that he has conquered and cleared, sowed and tilled. He invites us to a share at the hour of the harvest.

The society of intelligent minds is always an exclusive society; reading gives us easier entrance to it. We cast on the inspired page an imploring glance that is not in vain; we are helped, paths are opened up to us; we are reassured, initiated; the work of God in rare minds is put to our account as well as to theirs; we grow through them; we are enriched through them; the giant carries the dwarf, and the ancestor offers us an inheritance. Shall we not profit by these resources? We can if we will. Attention and fidelity are all that is necessary.

Genius makes all things new for us. Genius is a seer, whose pre-eminent gift it is to present reality to our minds under an unsuspected light, in the heart of a connected system which is a sort of new creation—that reality which was there, obvious, and which we did not see.

The whole infinity of thought lies behind every fact; but we wait for the vision to be revealed to us. Genius all alone steps forward, draws aside the veils and says: Come! Science—*scientia*—consists in seeing into things; genius does see into things; it moves freely in the intimate heart of created beings, and, thanks to it, Being itself speaks to us, instead of our own feeble and uncertain echoes.

Genius simplifies things. Most great discoveries are a sudden lightning-flash of concentrated thought. Great maxims are a condensation of multiple experiences. The sublime touch in painting, music, architecture, poetry, is a burst of inspiration which holds and unifies values previously scattered and indeterminate.

A great man, because he reflects common humanity, gives us the essence of its attainments, just as Leonardo da Vinci reduced to the synthesis of a single moment the changing expressions of his model. Genius is the Egyptian line applied to everything, and its rich simplicity furnishes forth our splendid display.

Genius stimulates us and gives us confidence. The stir it arouses is a spur to ardent personal endeavor, revealing a vocation, correcting overanxious timidity. A sense of sublimity breaks on our soul like a sunrise. Wisdom, tried and proved in her heroes, has whispered an invitation to us too; and what happiness it is to say: She is in me also!

It is perhaps not true that great men reflect only their age; but it is true that they reflect humanity, and every sharer in that humanity has his share of their glory. Malicious thinkers, looking at the human race, may say what they like: the existence of men of genius proves them wrong—as wrong as the Jews looking at Jesus when they said: "Can anything good come out of Nazareth?" Yes, some good can come out of our poor world, since a Plato did. A great man would be nothing if, by his resources and the use he makes of them, he were not a son of Man. Now the stock from which he springs has not lost its fertility; those in whom the same sap flows may always hope to grow and to produce in their turn immortal flowers.

The very errors of great men can contribute to the profit we expect to reap from associating with them. We have to be on our guard against them; in their strength they sometimes err; almost all of them have shadows, like a face with very marked features—the exaggeration of a point of view, or some other excess may carry them far from rectitude. Still, there is not one of them but in spite of aberrations leads a prepared mind to the eternal foundations of knowledge and the secrets of life.

Their errors are not vulgar errors, but excesses; in their very mistakes they are not without depth and keenness of vision; following them cautiously, one is sure to go a long way and one can avoid their blunders. "To them that love God, all things work together unto good," says the Apostle; for those who have a firm grasp of truth, everything can be useful. Having formed our mind under good teachers, keeping the framework of our thought well adjusted and firmly jointed, we may hope to grow through contact with the errors of genius. In this danger, provided we do not expose ourselves to it indiscreetly, there is even a grace; a new sphere is revealed to us; an aspect of the world is shown to us, perhaps too exclusively, but vividly; the stimulus given to our mind remains; the deepening required by the very act of resistance strengthens us; we shall be better formed, more effectually safeguarded, for having incurred these sublime risks without succumbing to them.

St. Thomas, whose idea I base myself on here, concludes from these observations that we owe gratitude even to those who have thus tested us, if because of them and their action we have made any kind of progress. Directly, we owe everything to truth alone, but indirectly we owe to those who are in error the mental development that, thanks to them, Providence provides for us.[1]

Think what the Church owes to heresies and philosophy to its great conflicts of opinion. If it had not been for Arius, Eutyches, Nestorius, Pelagius, Luther, Catholic dogma would not have been constituted. If Kant had not shaken the foundations of human knowledge, criteriology would still be in its childhood; and if Renan had not written on Christian origins, the Catholic clergy would be far from having the historical and exegetical formation they now possess.

What is true collectively is true individually. We must learn right thinking principally by contact

[1] St. Thomas, *In II. Metaphys. lect. I.*

with the wise; but folly itself contains a lesson; he who escapes its contagion draws strength from it. "He who stumbles without falling makes a bigger step forward."

V

An essential condition for profiting by our reading, whether of ordinary books or those of writers of genius, is to tend always to reconcile our authors instead of setting one against another. The critical spirit has its place; we may have to disentangle opinions and classify men; the method of contrast is then admissible and needs only not to be forced. But when the aim is formation of the mind, personal profit, or even a teacher's exposition, it is quite a different matter. In these cases it is not the thoughts, but the truths, that interest us; not men's disputes, but their work and what is lasting in it. It is futile to linger endlessly over differences; the fruitful research is to look for points of contact.

Here St. Thomas gives us an admirable example. He always tried to compare doctrines, to illustrate and complete them one by the other. He was an Aristotelian, but leaned also on Plato; without being an Augustinian he fed his mind constantly on Augustine; he who declared Averrhoes a corrupter of peripateticism, nevertheless calls him a sublime spirit (*praeclarum ingenium*), and quotes him constantly. When he comments on a passage, he interprets the text, if need be, so as to make it yield its purest content of truth or its greatest wealth of meaning, saying what we are to see in it, charitably closing his eyes to any regrettable aspect it may have. No one less than he resembles those proof-readers who read purely to find misprints.

The man who wants to acquire from his authors, not fighting qualities, but truth and penetration, must bring to them this spirit of conciliation and diligent harvesting, the spirit of the bee. Honey is made of many kinds of flowers. A method of exclusion, summary elimination, and narrow choice is infinitely harmful to a man's formation, and reveals in the mind that tends that way a defect which speaks badly for the future. "Every individual who is not creative," writes Goethe, "has a negative, narrow, exclusive taste and succeeds in depriving creative being of its energy and life." Such an intelligence grows narrow; instead of looking at everything from the point of view of the universal, it falls to the level of a spirit of clique and gossip.

It is not only on the doorsteps that we meet gossips; they are to be found in the history of philosophy, of the sciences, even of theology; and many people copy them. Rise above that. You who seek truth and are ready to recognize its countenance everywhere, do not set its servants up one against the other, even though they should be among those "incomplete angels," men of partial genius whom truth has visited without making its dwelling-place in them.

Especially in regard of very great minds it is a sort of profanation to adopt a fault-finding attitude. Let us regret their errors, but without violent condemnation; let us build bridges, not dig ditches between their doctrines. There is a great revelation in discovering the hidden links that exist between ideas and systems the most dissimilar. To address oneself to this work of reconstituting the integral truth out of its misinterpretations is far more fruitful than to be perpetually criticizing.

At bottom, if we know how to utilize great men, they all put us in touch with the same essential truths. I do not say that they all proclaim these truths, but they place them in our line of vision, lead or drive us invincibly toward them. They appear to be in conflict and to split up knowledge, to cause disunion in the human mind; in reality they converge. The columns of the temple have their separate bases on the pavement, they are spaced widely apart, they form distant bays; but the arches they bear converge, and by means of many moldings they join to form a single roof. The fulfilment of your desire is to see that sheltering roof and to take refuge beneath it—you who are seeking not notoriety, nor the clash of parties, nor the spirit of discussion, nor artificial stimulation of the intelligence, but truth alone.

VI

One last and capital point has to be noted about reading. The reader, if in a certain way he must be passive in order to open his mind to truth and not to hinder its ascendency over him, is nevertheless called on to react to what he reads so as to make it his own and by means of it to form his soul. We read only to think, we acquire wealth in order to use it, we eat to live.

We have condemned the eternal reader who little by little arrives at a mechanical output of mental activity, an intellectual automatism which ceases to be real work. But one need not be a great reader to slip into that passive habit. For many people books are like knitting. Their minds, sunk in a sort of indolence, watch the march-past of ideas and stand by inert, "Just as a drowsing shepherd sees the stream flow on." [1]

And yet work is life, life is assimilation, assimilation is a reaction of the living organism to nourishment. It is not enough to gather the harvest at the right time, to bind one's sheaf of grain and bake one's bread; one must fashion one's body with it, for that alone is the real use of the luxuriant wheat.

A man who is always listening may never learn, unless he changes into his own substance what he has heard in his docile intercourse with others. Docility is praiseworthy and necessary; it is not enough. "Obedience is at the foundation of progress," said Auguste Comte; but it is not progress. The man of genius who teaches us might say, like Him who inspires him: "I am come that they may have life and may have it more abundantly" (John 10:10). Will what was life in others be for us nothing more than a lamp whose light has died?

No one can teach us without our own effort. Reading puts truth before us; we have to make it ours. It is not the dealer in the market place who

[1] Alfred de Musset.

feeds my body. What I eat must turn into my substance: I alone can bring that about. "By doctrine," wrote Boethius, "the mind of man is only stimulated to know."[1] St. Augustine had said before him: "A man teaching is as the husbandman to the tree."[2]

St. Thomas, going more deeply into the question, observes that the spoken and written word do not even reach the mind directly; their whole function is by means of sounds and signs to supply the soul with matter. The sound rings out; the light vibrates; our senses perceive and pass on the signal; and, by an inverse movement this signal, springing from the idea, has the mission of awakening a similar idea. But in all that process, minds do not touch one another; the signals of one mind make only indirect contact with the other; and what produces knowledge is not the system of signs put before us, it is the work of our own reason on those signs.

At bottom, the intellectual propositions that are put to us remain as much outside our intelligence as the things themselves that we want to know; they have only this advantage, that they correspond, as signs, to ideas already worked out and set in order. That facilitates our thought but does not take its place. All that teaching does is to provide us with means of mental activity, as medicine offers our bodies means of getting well; but just as

[1] Boethius, *De Consolatione philosophiae,* V. prose 5.
[2] St. Augustine, Opusculum *De Magistro.*

no medicine can act on an inert organism, no teaching can succeed with a negligent mind.

In reality nature herself operates the cure; and the mind is enlightened only by its own light, unless we say: by the light of God infused into it according to the words of the Psalm: "The light of Thy countenance, O Lord, is signed upon us." (Ps. 4:7.) Indeed, in the last analysis, God is our only Master, He who speaks within us, and from Him within us all instruction comes; strictly speaking, thought is incommunicable from man to man.[1]

This penetrating analysis has practical consequences. If the idea does not reach us from without, if it is necessarily within us that it must come to birth, let us make it our endeavor that the intellectual matter provided by the book—those signals from a silent interlocutor—may really raise us to the thought expressed and even beyond it, for an idea evoked in an active mind should always rouse some further idea.

We enter into the intimacy of genius only by sharing the same inspiration; to listen from outside is to condemn oneself not to hear. It is not with the eyes, nor with the ears, that one hears a great saying, it is with a soul on the level of what is revealed to it, with an intelligence illuminated by one and the same light.

The source of knowledge is not in books, it is in reality, and in our thought. Books are signposts;

[1] St. Thomas, *De Magistro,* in the *Quaestiones disputatae de Veritate,* q.XI, art. I, with the arguments and answers.

the road is older, and no one can make the journey to truth for us.

It is not what a writer says that is of first importance to us; the important thing is what *is*. Our mind has the task not of repeating but of comprehending—that is, we must "take with" us, *cum-prehendere,* we must vitally assimilate, what we read, and we must finally think for ourselves. When we have heard the words, we must, after the author and perhaps thanks to him but in the last resort independently of him, compel our own soul to re-express them. We must recreate for our own use the sum total of knowledge.

In any case the principal profit from reading, at least from reading great works, is not the acquisition of scattered truths, it is the increase of our wisdom. Amiel, comparing the French with the German mind, said: "The Germans bring the bundles of wood to the woodpile; the French provide the sparks." That judgment is perhaps too absolute; but certainly it is the sparks that start the flame.

To develop wisdom was the first object of our education; it is still that of the education that we essay to provide for ourselves. Without wisdom, what we take in would be worthless, it would be as useless as was the first when it was on the library shelf. In ourselves also there are volumes and texts of great value that we do not read.

What an abuse it is to associate with great minds and to get from them nothing but formulas! And how clearly it will appear when, in writing ourselves, we want to utilize them! Such parroting is speedily seen for what it is, and it is soon evident that the writer is a nobody.

To make real use of another is invention. Even when one quotes literally, if the passage is introduced in a setting in which it has its exact place, and if the setting is on the same level, is of a piece and makes a living unity with what it borrows, one is showing an originality equal in a sense to the master's. The glory given to another redounds to oneself. The quotation is in this case like the word one finds in the dictionary, but which one still creates as the soul creates the body.

That is how St. Thomas, Bossuet, Pascal, quote. And we who aspire to quite humble tasks must apply to them the same laws of the mind. Truth is all men's ancestor; wisdom addresses her invitation to all; we must not leave to the greatest the monopoly of making a superior use of what is offered us. Compared with men of genius we are only children, but we are children with an inheritance. What they give us is ours because it belongs to eternity; from eternity they themselves received it. We must contemplate, while they speak to us, what was before them and is above them, what God makes ready for us all.

It is on these conditions that we may attain originality; and we may count fully, if some day our wisdom grows, on doing original work in the true sense of the term. If we are to produce something truly ours, reading can only serve to stimulate us—to enrich our personality, not our pages. That is in another sense what I said, about finding in books what is not in them, finding a way of entry through them into new domains.

If it is true that it is only by our work that we acquire ordinary knowledge, it is still more evidently true that we cannot make our contribution of new thought to the world except by our own effort. I should like, when I read, to find some happy suggestion, some starting-point for a fresh train of ideas in my book; but then to lay it down as soon as possible, to shake myself free with a feeling of indebtedness. It is my duty to be myself. What is the good of repeating others? However unimportant I am, I know that God makes none of His spiritual beings without a purpose—He does not make the least natural object without a purpose. I am obeying my Master by setting myself free. I am alive, I am not a mere reflection, and I want to live a fruitful life. Whatever engenders nothing is non-existent; my reading must enable me to engender thought in the likeness, not of the author who inspires me, but of myself!

That is, I think, the last word on the question of books. A book is a signal, a stimulant, a helper, an initiator—it is not a substitute and it is not a chain. Our thought must be what we ourselves are. When we read, our masters must not be a goal for us, but a starting-point. A book is a cradle, not a tomb. Physically we are born young and we die old; intellectually, because of the heritage of the ages, "we are born old; we must try to die young." [1]

Men of real genius do not want to pinion us, but to make us free. But if they did aim at enslaving us, we should have to resist them, to be on our guard against an invasion of our liberty that would be so much the more destructive as we have not equal resources for the struggle. We must emancipate our soul. The more our thought springs from our inner depths, from what is incommunicable in us, the more it will reflect man, and the more readily will other men recognize themselves in it. Human respect loses touch with humanity, spontaneity gets near to it. Repetition of others' thoughts, whether open or disguised, soon proves wearisome. "If you speak of nothing but what you have read," says Schopenhauer, "no one will read you."

In fine, let us work with truth for our companion, with God for our companion. Our model is in the creative Thought. Men of genius are but a shadow. To be the shadow of a shadow is a poor thing for one, who, whether small or great, is here on earth a spiritual entity, incomparable, unparalleled, unique.

Man is multiple and each of us is a separate specimen of mankind; God is in all men; let us have the wisdom to honor man and to respect God in ourselves.

[1] A thought familiar to Abbé de Tourville, who applied it to social science.

The Management of Memory

I. *What Things Are to be Remembered*
II. *In What Order They Are to be Remembered*
III. *How They Can be Remembered*

I

It would be no use to acquire knowledge by reading, and reflection would be impossible, if memory did not retain and present to us at the opportune moment whatever is to be of service to our work and to our mental operations.

Many great men were endowed with prodigious memories, others were deficient in this respect; the majority had indifferent memories and were obliged to make up for the limitation in various ways. One cannot class the great masters by this faculty; but it is nevertheless certain that, other things being equal, a richly filled and tenacious memory is a precious resource.

Let us not conclude that we must exercise the memory indiscriminately and load our minds with the greatest possible number of notions, facts, images, passages from books. It might seem that St. Thomas recommends this, when he writes in his *Sixteen Precepts:* "Lay up in the treasury of your mind all that you can, like a man aiming at filling a vessel." We must understand this brief maxim with an implied reservation. We must remember everything that we can, on condition that it is useful, as with the same reservation we read everything we can.

We have put the intellectual on his guard against the abuse of reading. Our objections on that score apply largely here also, seeing that remembering means preserving acquisitions inseparable both from their advantages and their harmfulness.

All our masters tell us that to overload the memory is injurious to personal thought and to attention. The mind gets bogged in the mass of its material; what it does not use encumbers and paralyzes it; the dead weight oppresses the living personality; excessive food is a poison—we have the proof of it in the great number of people with pretensions to erudition whose minds are warped and inactive, in so many of those we call "living libraries" and "walking dictionaries."

We do not live by memory, we use our memory to live. Engrave on your mind whatever can help you to conceive or carry out a project, whatever your soul can assimilate, whatever can serve your purpose, vivify your inspiration, and sustain your work. As for the rest, consign it to oblivion. And if it is possible that on occasion many things may be useful which did not seem likely to be so, and in fact are not usually so, that is not a reason for saying: let us remember them on the off-chance. If need be you will look them up again; they will easily be preserved on paper. On the pretext that you may have to catch any train, you do not learn the Railway Guide by heart.

Pascal said that he did not think he had ever forgotten a thing that he wanted to remember;

that is the right sort of memory, on condition that one wants to remember only what is useful. When St. Augustine defines happiness as "desiring nothing but the good and having all that one desires," he is equally defining the best kind of memory. Entrust to yours all that is good, ask God to give you if He will the grace of Pascal, that of St. Thomas "in whom nothing went to waste," or that of Mozart who after one hearing reproduced a whole solemn Mass. But I repeat that such a grace is not necessary; one can supply its place without suffering any real harm. And what is the good of trying to estimate its value seeing that we have to make use of what has been given us, not of what we lack!

It is a capital rule to bring the memory into the general current of our intellectual life, to make it share in our vocation. Memory, like the mind itself, should specialize; in the same degree, with the same concentration on the principal object, and the same broad outlook on secondary matters.

There are things that everyone must know, that in particular every Catholic must keep in mind; there are things that an intellectual cannot afford to be ignorant of; there are others connected more or less closely with our special subject that each person will feel the need of possessing according to the breadth or narrowness of mind that he brings to them; lastly there are things essentially belonging to our special subject, without which we are beneath our task and properly accused of ignorance and culpable inertia.

What each one must try to keep in the forefront of his mind and available at a moment's need is what forms the basis of his work, what for that reason all the eminent men in his calling know. In this matter no negligence is permissible, and these things should be acquired with the least possible delay. The rest of what is required for a particular task will be picked up by degrees, without too much effort to fix it permanently.

In both cases it is clear that the mental recording starts from a preconceived idea, as our reading does; there is only this difference, that a particular piece of work is the vocation of the moment, while our vocation is lasting work, and the memory adapts itself to each.

Nicole suggests to the religious man "to learn by heart various psalms and texts of Holy Scripture, in order to sanctify the memory by these divine words." [1] It is a way of setting the seal on the heavenly vocation common to all of us, and of facilitating our effort after good. Nowadays very few people understand such advice. A man will declaim long passages from Virgil, Racine, Musset, who would be hard put to it to recite a psalm, who does not know his *Angelus,* his *Salve Regina,* his *Te Deum,* or *Magnificat.* That is evidently out of order. What is riveted in our mind by memory has more effect on us; a Catholic must desire that effect to be greatest with regard to what enlivens his faith. It would help him so much if he could from time to time during the day or when occasion arises re-

[1] *Op. cit.* p. 261.

peat to himself forms of words full of Christian faith and devotion!

II

Having once settled how much is to be remembered, we must think of the order to be adopted. One's memory must not be chaos. Science–*scientia* –is knowledge through causes; the worth of every experience depends on its connections, its grouping with other experiences, its place in a graded scale of values. Merely to accumulate recollections is to make them all unusable and inevitably to recover them only by chance.

It is obvious that an intellectual memory should have the characteristics of intellectuality. Now, the intellect is not satisfied with a medley of notions that have no precise affinities. Look always for what connects this thing with that, what conditions are necessary for this and for that; let this coordination, and not scattered fragments, fix itself in your memory. A well-ordered mind is like a genealogical tree, in which all the branches spring from the trunk and so communicate with one another; relationships of every degree appear clearly in it, showing family descent in all its connections and as a whole.

That means that in memory, as in thought itself, we must bring everything into relation with what is essential. The primordial, the fundamental, the simple, whence complexity arises step by step and through successive *differences*, is what supports memory, as it does knowledge, and makes it efficient at the moment when it has to come into play.

It is of no use to have acquired myriads of notions, if our primary notions, instead of being enriched by the dependent points that memory reveals in them, are simply obstructed by these, and remain more utterly and fatally alone. Fifty data are no better than one, if they all stand only in the same relation to the fundamental idea; uncoordinated they remain fruitless, and like the fig tree in the Gospel they merely cumber the ground.

Hold fast above all—as we have said that we must seek above all—the leading conceptions; let them be always present at call, ready to throw light on everything new that comes before you, to keep the old ideas in their place in spite of new material; let these conceptions themselves grow and expand with every progress, as the brain profits by food entering the stomach, the heart by the exercise of the limbs.

A new idea acts retrospectively; a torch throws its light behind as well as before. Materials that were laid aside take on a new aspect when they are classified by means of an idea. Then everything within us is reborn and animated with a new life. But for that to happen, the paths of light must be open, our thoughts must be in order and linked consecutively one with another.

When we have put order in mind and memory, we shall be almost automatically protected from excessive strain, and we shall notice that two apparently distinct precepts are, as it were, but one. What is useless, what finds room in chaos, finds none in an organized whole. It must either serve, or go! There is something ridiculous in the effort made by a thing, as by a person, to intrude into an arrangement where it has no place, which it does not complete or serve. Every hierarchy sees to the policing of its own domain.

Thus relieved of useless burdens and properly ordered, the mind will be able to devote itself to its work with all its strength; it will go straight to what bears on its purpose and will not waste time over trifles; though these, it is true, may be the principal object of attention for someone else.

When Pasteur arrived in the South to combat the disease threatening French sericulture, which he was soon to overcome, he did not know the habits of the silkworm; he asked some rather casual questions of the great entomologist Henri Fabre. Fabre was surprised at first at the apparent superficiality of the "Parisian"; but soon, seeing that Pasteur was going deeper and working on the very springs of life, he understood, and later he praised this singlemindedness of genius.

There are in every subject-matter a few ideas that govern the whole, that are keys to everything; there are some also that govern life, and before these we must light the sanctuary lamp within our hearts.

The creative faculty largely depends on the wisdom and controlled activity of the memory. A firm grip of what is essential leaves the outlook open along every path, and what has been acquired tends to grow logically by taking up new matter. Thoughts become the starting-point of new thoughts; water flows into the river; rich people can always borrow; to everyone that hath shall be given and he shall abound, declares the Gospel. Every truth is the dawn of another; every possibility seeks its realization, and when interior order is ready to profit by new experience, it is like a root piercing deep down into the earth: its substance gets active; its fibres spread and drink in nourishing juices; life develops because the adaptation of the living thing to its setting is the single condition of its fertility, as it is at the outset of its substance.

The setting of our knowledge is the cosmos; and this is itself organization, structure. In order that the man of study may make progress it is necessary, and it suffices, that he should set up in himself, thanks to memory, a corresponding structure which enables him to adapt himself and thereby to act.

III

It remains to say how such a memory can be acquired, and how it can be turned to account. That is not a very great secret, although it is bound up with the most fundamental conditions of the life of our mind.

St. Thomas proposes four rules: (1) To set in order what one wants to remember; (2) to apply the mind deeply to it; (3) to think over it often; (4) when one wants to recollect it, to take the chain of connections by one end, which will bring the rest with it.[1] He adds accessorily, following Cicero, that it is a good thing to connect the memory of intellectual things with that of sensible things, for these latter, he says, are the proper object of the intellect and belong to memory of themselves, the others indirectly, by accident.[2]

The importance of order has already been stressed from another point of view; but everyone has probably had experience of its efficacy for fixing a recollection. A string of unconnected words, numbers, ideas, or elements is hard to get into our heads; these isolated notions do not settle in; each is, as it were, lost and promptly vanishes. On the contrary, a series holds together and has power of resistance. Anything that rests on its own proper reason and its natural group, that is rooted in its setting, runs less risk of being lost. A thing must exist in order to be preserved, and an element separated from its kindred elements only half exists.

So when you want to remember, notice the connections and the reasons of things; analyze them, look for the why and wherefore, observe the genealogy of happenings, their order of succession, and their dependent consequences; imitate the procedure of mathematics in which necessity starts from the axiom and arrives at the most distant conclusions. Fully to understand a thing, then to learn and to introduce into one's mind not frag-

[1] *De Memoria et Reminiscentia,* Lect. 5.
[2] *Ibid.,* Lect. 2.

ments, not loose links but a chain, is to make sure of the sticking quality of the whole. Union is strength.

The mental application recommended in the second place has for its purpose to make us lean heavily on the mysterious graving-tool which traces the shape of words and things within us. The keener our attention is, the more deeply are the lines engraved, and the better they will resist the continual flux which tends to replace ideas, as death replaces beings, by others. When you read or listen with a view to learning, be wholly present and concentrated; repeat to yourself as if aloud what is said to you; accent every syllable. I am speaking figuratively; but sometimes there are advantages in doing it literally. Be ready, as soon as you have read or heard the thing, to repeat it exactly in as far as you want to fix it in your memory. If it is a book, do not leave it without being able to sum it up and to estimate its value. I add this last suggestion, because the object that has roused us to active intervention is much less fugitive; it has a link with our personality.

Next, a necessity following on the previous one is to reflect, as often as is possible and as is worthwhile, on the object to be preserved from oblivion. Life obliterates the traces of life, and for that reason we were advised to engrave deeply; the same motive urges us, seeing that nevertheless the traces grow dimmer, to run the tool over the lines again, to apply plenty of acid to the etching, that is, constantly to revivify our useful thoughts and to ruminate on the facts that we want to keep before our eyes.

Agitation of mind is opposed to this operation, and therefore a peaceful life, passion-free, is necessary for the good use of memory as for all the intellectual functions.

The faculties of admiration, and youth of soul in face of nature and life, also contribute to memory. We retain better what has struck us. For this reason along with many others, the intellectual should cultivate that sense of the newness, the freshness of things, which is the starting-point for a vigorous urge towards fruitful creation or research.

Lastly, if we want to recall a memory and to revive old images, we are advised once again to take advantage of that fact of mutual dependence between thoughts and impressions on which we have based the constitution of our memory. Everything is more or less linked together in the brain even without our willing it; when we have willed it with all our power and diligently established the most natural connections possible between notions, we shall reap the profit.

We must not then search at random in a whole which was not formed at random; we must proceed logically, utilizing the logic of things as it reveals itself inescapably or as we have conceived it in the beginning; going up or down the series we have formed, making use of contiguous ideas, of circumstances; in short, bringing back deliberately under the pencil-beam of attention what attention had fixed and stored up according to its laws.

That is what St. Thomas calls pulling on the chain, and the end of the chain that he advises us to take hold of is that which presents itself as most immediately dependent on what we are seeking. For example: I remember that I thought of a plan of study; the plan escapes my memory; but I know that at the moment I was in such a place, or that I was talking to such a friend, or that it was connected with such a group of mental operations, such an aspect of my vocation; or again that my plan had been inspired by some previous reading, or was made necessary by some preceding work. To recover the vanished idea, I will recall the impression of the place, the friendly company, the group of ideas to which this one belonged, the part it was to play, the book that had been analyzed or the work done. Starting from that point, I will explore in every direction, and by various efforts I will try to find what I know was linked with one or other of these circumstances.

To sum up, what matters about memory is not so much the number of things it retains, as, first, their quality, then their order, and lastly skill in using them. Materials are hardly ever lacking to thought; it is thought that is lacking to the materials. To learn is nothing at all without intelligent assimilation, orderly connection, the progressive unity of a rich and well-ordered soul.

What is interesting is not the workyard, it is the

structure, and most of all the spirit of the dweller in the house. Keep your inspiration lofty, your attention keen; be sensitively responsive to truth, be eager in research, and you will remember enough.

NOTES

I. *How to Take Notes*
II. *How to Classify Notes*
III. *How to Use One's Notes*

I

We are obliged to repeat ourselves often. If we do it most of all in speaking of reading, memory, and notes, it is because these three subjects are in a sense one and the same. Through all three we aim at completing ourselves, so as to produce our work when the time comes.

We must read relatively little; we must remember very much less and anyhow nature sees to that. Notes, which are a sort of external memory, a "paper memory" Montaigne called them, must bear a very small proportion to reading; but they can cover more ground than memory, they can supply for it, and so take the strain off it and help our work in a measure that is hard to assign.

If we had to trust memory to keep intact and ready for use all that we have come upon or found out in the course of our life of study, it would be perfectly disastrous. Memory is an unreliable servant; it loses things, it buries them, it does not answer at call. We refuse to overload it, to cumber the mind; we prefer liberty of soul to a wealth of unusable ideas. The notebook or card index gets us out of our difficulty.

Moreover, memory in its way classifies things, and we have tried to help it; but its classifications are capricious and unstable. To remember the right thing at the right moment would take a degree of self-mastery that no mortal possesses. Here again notebooks and pigeonholes will help us. We must organize our reserves, lodge our savings in the bank where, it is true, they will yield no interest, but where they will at any rate be safe and ready at call. We ourselves shall be the cashiers.

Methods are very diverse in this matter; but there are certain general rules that it is useful to recall, so that each one can be guided by them.

We can distinguish two kinds of notes, corresponding to the remote and the immediate preparation for our work. You read or reflect in order to form and feed your mind; ideas occur that it seems good to fix in the memory; you come across facts, various indications, which may be useful later on; you note them down.

On the other hand, when you have to study a precise subject, to produce a definite piece of work, you try to gather material, you read what has been published on the question, you have recourse to all the sources of information at your disposal, you make your own reflections, and you do it all pen in hand.

Notes in the first category have the character of

being rather haphazard; the general outlines of your special study and the wise regulation of your reading can alone lessen the fortuitous element in them. As life is always complex, as the mind flits from subject to subject, as we ourselves have pleaded for broad interests, there is a great deal of chance about this sort of note. On the contrary, when you take notes with a view to producing something, as your projected work has a definite character so the notes grow definite also, they closely follow the subject before you and form a more or less organic whole. For these two sets of notes there are common rules, and special rules.

In both cases excess is to be avoided—such a congestion of material as to overwhelm us afterwards and be quite unusable. Some people have so many and such full notebooks that they are prevented by a sort of anticipatory discouragement from ever opening them. Their imaginary treasures have cost much time and trouble, and they yield no return; they are choked up by a vast number of worthless things; the useful ones might often with advantage have stayed in the tomes from which they were extracted, a reference with a rapid summary taking the place of wearisome pages.

Keep notes made after thinking, and with moderation. In order to avoid first-minute surprises, the effect of some passing preoccupation, or the enthusiasm sometimes aroused by a brilliant form of words, do not definitely include the passage in your notes without letting some time elapse. Quietly, at the right distance, you will judge of the value of your harvest and store up only the good grain in your barns.

In both cases equally, we must make our notes after vigorous mental work with a sense of our personal needs. The aim is to complete oneself, to furnish one's own mind, to provide oneself with armor suited to one's own person, and to the requirements of the battle to be fought. Even if a thing is all very well in its own way, even if it is valuable in theory, that is not a reason for transcribing it. Thank God there are many fine things in books; will you therefore copy down the whole National Library? You do not buy a coat because it is handsome, but because it suits you; and a piece of furniture that you admire in the curio shop had better stay there if in size and style it is not right for the house you want to furnish.

Avoid caprice in everything. Just as reading is food, and memory a rich possession that becomes part of the personality, notes also are storehouses of nourishment and of personality. Reading, memory, notes should all complete us, should therefore be like us, have something of our self, our rôle, our vocation; they should correspond to what we are aiming at and to the form of external activity by which we can and will realize it.

Everyone knows how much an account book tells about its owner, his way of living and the objects he pursues; the notebooks and the pigeonholes should be just as closely related to the intellectual, to what he must be and wants to be; in them is his credit account, at least in part; and that account must correspond both to its owner and to his probable expenditure. I am reflected in my work; I must also be reflected in the means I use, if I have adapted them wisely to the work and to myself.

Better still, it would be desirable that besides documentation properly so-called—facts, texts, or statistics—the notes you take should be not only suited to you, but should be your own, and that they should be your own not only when they emanate from your thinking but also when they arise out of reading. Reading itself should awaken reflection, and we have already said that a borrowed passage can become our own to the point of not differing at all from an original creation.

I read, and I write while reading; but I write down what I think after contact with someone else, more than I write down that other person's thought; and my ideal is that that should be true even if, not hoping better to express our common thought, I transcribe textually. A writer is a man who conceives an idea; but I also conceive whatever I assimilate profoundly, what I endeavor to penetrate, to comprehend in the full sense of the word, what I make my own; I am therefore the writer also, and I store the thing up as part of my own wealth.

As to notes taken remotely, there is nothing else essential to consider. Proximately, with a view to a particular work, we must intensify the application of our rules, and add another.

We asked that the mode of notation should be personal, that is, in exact relation to the writer; it must further be in strict relation to the work in hand. You have a precise object; think hard about it; let your mind trace out, if necessary, a provisional plan according to which you will guide your reading and your thinking, according to which also you will note down one thing or another that fits into its subdivisions. Claude Bernard declared that a scientific observation is the answer to a question set by the mind to itself, and that in reality one only finds what one is looking for. In the same way, something that we read intelligently is a possible answer to the question set within our mind by the subject to be treated; we must therefore read with a feeling of expectation, as, at the exit gate of a railway station, we keep our eyes fixed on the stream of travellers among whom there is a friend.

Let your reading then be more and more influenced by a definite idea; let it take account not only of your vocation and your personality, but of their immediate application. Reading in that way has a set purpose; now, a set purpose is like a sieve which retains the desired grain and lets the rest slip through. Do not let your attention wander; do not linger by the way; have only your own objective before your eyes, without regard to that of the author which may be quite different. I venture to say, even though the expression has something repugnant about it and is almost always a warning: put on blinkers, so as better to concentrate on the task that at this precise moment should absorb you entirely.

There are two somewhat different methods of work, which may perhaps have to be used turn by turn according to the nature of your study.

You can draw up a detailed plan and seek your documentation afterwards. You can begin with the documentation, thinking and reading along a line which evidently presupposes certain guiding ideas, but without a plan properly so-called. In this case you read round about the subject, you look at it in every aspect, you take soundings in an effort to leave no part of it unexplored; a plan begins to shape itself and you jot down the ideas like Pascal when he writes the word order at the head of a fragment; you put aside the passages that can be used as they stand; you determine the ideas that you will have to develop, noting down only their principal characteristics if these present themselves; you record the precise expressions, the felicitous comparisons that occur to you; sometimes you develop a whole passage, not with the intention of completing it, but because it comes of itself and because inspiration is like grace, which passes by and does not come back.

When you think you have explored the whole ground, I mean as regards what you are aiming at or hoping for, your work is prepared; the workshop is full of materials of which some are quite in the rough, others provisionally shaped out. We shall speak presently of the work of construction;

but it is already clear in this case that the plan will spring from the materials, not the materials from the plan.

This procedure, which seems the less logical and abstractly speaking is indeed so, has the advantage of leaving you freer in your thoughts and preliminary studies, of opening up the way more fully to inspiration, of keeping you in joy, because you make discoveries without forcing yourself to look precisely for them, because you can go forwards, and backwards, leave off a while, wait for the right vein, and work only when you are fresh, without mental constraint.

A work may thus be finished before it is begun; all its value is determined in your notes; the plan is there latent, the preliminary adjustable sketch of the architect, permitting various combinations; but the matter is grasped, mastered, and you are sure that when the plan does emerge, it will correspond to a real conception, to ideas that you have, not to ideas that you are running after—that it will therefore be no arbitrary diagrammatic scheme, no system of compartments to be filled even though you may have nothing natural, spontaneous, and therefore really living to put into them.

Notes of this kind, notes of study, notes of inspiration cannot be made in odd moments; they are intense work, and it should be reserved for what we have called the moments of plenitude to look for them. Other notes, although they too require effort, will sometimes be of the nature of a happy find, will come by chance. But those will be best that deep study invites you to gather in like a harvest, and to store up as the wealth of life.

II

Having made your notes and supposing you think them likely to be of use later on, you must classify them. In business, order is money, and what an amount of money! In the life of the mind, order is thought. It is useless to make a note if you cannot find it again at the right moment; in that case, it would be merely a buried treasure. To keep some trace of one's reading and of one's reflections, to make extracts from sources of documentary information, is a good thing; but on condition that one is thus enabled to turn back and open the favorite author at will, and to turn back and open the book of one's own experience also.

We must beware of a certain craze for collecting which sometimes takes possession of those who make notes. They want to have a full notebook or filing cabinet; they are in a hurry to put something in the empty spaces, and they accumulate passages as other people fill stamp and postcard albums. That is a deplorable practice; it is a sort of childishness, and risks becoming a mania. Order is a necessity, but it must serve us, not we it. To indulge obstinately in accumulating and completing is to turn one's mind away from producing and even from learning; excessive attention to classification interferes with use; now in this connection everything must be subordinated to the good of the work.

How are notes to be classified? Famous men have adopted different systems. The best, in the long run, is the system that one has tried, tested by one's own needs and intellectual habits, and established by long practice.

The plan of having a book in which the notes collected are written or pasted consecutively is very defective, because it allows of no classification, even with the help of leaving blank spaces of which the extent cannot be foreseen. Different books for each subject remedy this drawback to some extent, but even that does not permit exact classification; and besides the notes do not readily lend themselves to use at the moment of writing.

One can have strong paper folders bearing a title, to hold the notes of a particular category. A collection of such folders, under a more general title, can be kept in a rack or cabinet; and each compartment will bear on the outside, if not the title which one may prefer not to display, at any rate a serial number corresponding to a table of contents that the worker will always have at hand.

But it seems by far the most practical method, for most kinds of work, to keep notes on slips. Have a supply of slips of fairly strong paper, of a uniform size that you will decide on according to the average length of your notes. There will be nothing to prevent you from continuing on a second slip the extract begun on the first. Your slips must be cut exactly, with a paper-cutter; any binder or printer will do it for you in five minutes; and besides there are special firms that will spare you the trouble, providing slips of every size and color as well as the necessary boxes and accessories. For of course, if your collection of notes is to be of any size, you will need boxes or a cabinet with drawers of appropriate dimensions. You will also need a certain number of tagged slips, guide-cards, so as to number each category visibly after having numbered each slip, in the corner or in the middle.

Starting from that point, here is the procedure to be followed. When you make a note while reading, or thinking of your work, or in bed, etc., make it on a slip; or if you have none at hand, on a smaller bit of paper, on one side only, which you will paste on to a slip later. Having written your slip, you will put it in its place, unless you decide to wait awhile, according to the advice we gave a little way back.

Classification presupposes that you have adopted a carefully chosen method suitable to your work. Here we can only make general suggestions. Each person should draw up, if necessary, a catalog of subjects with divisions and subdivisions, about which he already has, or thinks that he must procure, notes. There is a very ingenious system, called the decimal system, applicable to every kind of research: I refer for its elucidation to a booklet that is interesting and very clear.[1]

If one fears complication, which is indeed a grave drawback, let each one fall back on his own practical ideas. In this matter we must be realists,

[1] *L'Organisation du Travail intellectuel*, by Dr. Chavigny, Fellow of the Val de Grâce. Delagrave, 1918.

and not amuse ourselves by establishing *a priori* divisions which would be quite useless.

According to your catalog, if you have made one, in which every division or subdivision bears a serial letter or number, you can put your slips in order. When they are once arranged, you will find them again without any trouble at the moment of work.

III

You have now come to the time for using your documentation. You have your immediate collection, notes taken in view precisely of the present work; and besides, you have in reserve, not yet drawn on, old notes that have a more or less direct bearing on it. Get the whole lot together, referring if necessary to your catalog and the indications it gives you. Then, according to what we have already said, two ways are open to you.

If you have a detailed plan, and if your notes have been made or sought with reference to it, number the successive headings of your plan. Number correspondingly (lightly in pencil if the notes are to be used again later) the slips that relate to them; put together the slips bearing the same numbers; insert each little bundle in a clip; sort out the bundles, and all you have then to do is to write, laying out before you in succession the contents of each bundle.

If, on the contrary, you have prepared your work without a settled plan, simply following general lines, you must now draw up your plan; you must extract it from the documents themselves. For that purpose, you may proceed as follows. You have all your slips loose; take them one by one and write on a sheet of paper, in order, the contents of each, making the briefest possible summary. When you have gone all through the stock of notes, you have before your eyes the ideas at your disposal. Look through them to find out how they are connected or interdependent; pick out mentally the leading ideas; arrange the subordinate points under each; to help yourself in that, use marginal numbers which can be changed as often as is necessary. Little by little light will break and order will emerge from the confused mass.

Then copy out your brief summaries in the order you have attained, the numbers being now consecutive. If there are gaps in your plan, fill them in; if necessary you will do some supplementary research on these points; number with a number corresponding to each theme the slips referring to it; sort and clip as before, and your work is prepared.

chapter 8

Creative Work

I. *Writing*
II. *Detachment from Self and the World*
III. *Constancy, Patience, and Perseverance*
IV. *Doing Things Well and Finishing Everything*
V. *Attempting Nothing beyond One's Powers*

I

You have come now to the moment for producing results. One cannot be forever learning and forever getting ready. Moreover, learning and getting ready are inseparable from a certain amount of production, which is helpful to them. One finds one's way only by taking it. All life moves in a circle. An organ that is used grows and gets strong; a strong organ can be used more effectively. You must write throughout the whole of your intellectual life.

In the first place one writes for oneself, to see clearly into one's personal position and problems, to give definition to one's thoughts, to keep up and stimulate attention which sometimes flags if not kept on the alert by activity—to make a beginning on lines of investigation which prove to be necessary as one writes, to encourage oneself in an effort that would be wearisome in the absence of some visible result, lastly to form one's style and acquire that possession which puts the seal on all the others, the writer's art.

When you write, you must publish, as soon as good judges think you capable of it and you yourself feel some aptitude for that flight. The young bird knows when he can venture into space; his mother knows it more surely. Relying on yourself and on a wise maternity of the spirit, fly as soon as you can.

Contact with the public will compel you to do better; well-deserved praise will stimulate you; criticism will try out your work; you will be, as it were, forced to make progress instead of stagnating, which might be the result of perpetual silence. To father some intellectual work is to sow a good and fruitful seed. Every work is a wellspring.

Père Gratry insists strongly on the efficacy of writing. He would like people always to meditate pen in hand; and to devote the untroubled morning hour to this contact of the mind with itself. We must take account of varying individual dispositions; but it is certain that for the majority of people, the pen as it runs plays the part of the trainer at games.

To speak is to listen to one's soul and to the truth within it. To speak alone and wordlessly, as one does by writing, is to listen and perceive truth with a freshness of sensation like that of a man who rises in the early morning and holds his ear to nature.

Everything must have a beginning. "The beginning is more than the half of the whole," said Aristotle. If you produce nothing you get a habit of passivity; timidity grows continually and the fear caused by pride; you hesitate, waste your powers in waiting, become as unproductive as a knotted tree-bud.

I have said that the art of writing requires long and early application and that this gradually becomes a mental habit and constitutes what is called style. My style, my pen, is the intellectual instrument which I use to express myself and to tell others what I understand of eternal truth. This instrument is a quality of my being, an interior bent, a disposition of the living brain, that is, it is a particular evolution of my self. "Style is the man."

Therefore in each person the style is formed according as the writer himself is formed; silence is a diminution of the personality. If you want fully to exist from the intellectual point of view, you must know how to think aloud, to think explicitly, that is to shape both within you and for the outside world the word which is the expression of your mind.

Perhaps it is in place here to say briefly what style should be if it is to correspond to the aim we have been suggesting to the intellectual.

Alas! In order to venture to say how to write, one should oneself abstain. It is not difficult to be humble when one has fallen under the spell of a master style, or experienced the resulting sense of liberation and expansion in reading, say Pascal,

La Fontaine, Bossuet, Montaigne. One can at least acknowledge the idea one is aiming at and falling short of; to describe it is to admit one's shortcomings, but it does one honor to prize what passes judgment on one's own writing.

The qualities of style may be set out under as many headings as you will; but they can all be contained, I think, in these three words: truth, individuality, and simplicity; unless you prefer to sum it all up in a single formula; one must write *truly*.

A style is true when it corresponds to a necessity of thought and when it keeps intimate contact with things.

The expression of thought in word is an act of life: it must not stand for a clean cut in life, which is what happens when we fall into artificiality, conventionality, what M. Bergson would call the "ready-made." To write with one part of one's being, to live one's sincere and spontaneous life with another, is an insult to the spoken word and to the harmonious unity of human nature.

The ceremonial discourse is the type of those things that are said because they have to be said, in which the thought is merely an effort at apt expression, an expenditure of that eloquence which is the laughingstock of genuine eloquence.[1] And indeed the ceremonial discourse is often but a mere

[1] One of Pascal's *Thoughts* which may be paraphrased: truly spontaneous and inspired eloquence mocks at the eloquence which is based on rules of rhetoric, has no need of or use for them. (Tr. Note.)

passing impersonal thing. There may be genius in it—Demosthenes and Bossuet are examples; but that only happens if the occasion draws from our substance something that would in any case surge up of itself, something connected with our habitual outlook, our constant meditations.

The virtue of the word, spoken or written, is abnegation and sincerity: abnegation which puts our personality aside lest it mar the exchange between truth speaking within and the listening soul; sincerity which expresses simply what inspiration has revealed, with no addition of verbiage.

"Look in thy heart and write," said Sidney. The man who writes like that, without pride or artifice, as if it were for himself, is in reality speaking for humanity, provided he has the talent that will carry true words far and wide. Humanity will recognize itself in him, because it is human nature that has inspired the discourse. Life recognizes life. If I give my neighbor just black marks on white paper, he will perhaps look at the thing curiously, but then he will throw it down; if I am like a tree offering foliage and fruit full of rich sap, if I give my whole self, I will convince him, and like Pericles, leave the dart in men's souls.

If I obey the laws of thought, I cannot but show myself in close contact with things, or rather in the heart of things. Thinking is conceiving what is; writing truly, that is writing according to one's thought, is revealing what is, not stringing sentences together. And so the secret of writing is to stand and study things ardently, until they speak to you and themselves determine their own expression.

Speech and writing must correspond to the truth of life. The listener is a man; the speaker must not be a shadow. The listener brings you a soul to heal or to enlighten; do not put him off with words. While you are developing your periods, he must be able to look outside himself and within himself, and to feel the correspondence with what you say.

Truth in style avoids the stereotyped expression, the cliché. A cliché is an old truth, a formula that has become common property, a set of words that once was fresh, and is no longer so precisely because it has lost contact with the reality whence it sprang—because it floats in the air, a silly foolish tinsel ornament that takes the place of a flow of living metal, of a direct and immediate transcription of the idea.

As Paul Valéry observes, it is automatic use that kills languages. We are alive, he says, when we use syntax "with full consciousness," taking trouble watchfully to bring out every element, avoiding certain effects that arise of themselves and obtrusively claim priority. That claim is precisely the reason for turning away these parasites, these intruders, these unwanted visitors.

Greatness of style consists in discovering the essential links between the elements of thought and in expressing them with an art that completely excludes every tentative approximation. What an ideal [1] that is which Emerson formulates, to write

[1] Quoted in the biography by Régis Michaud.

as the dew is deposited on the leaf, and stalactites on the walls of the grotto, as the flesh grows out of the blood, and the woody fiber of the tree is formed from the sap!

We said that the proud and disturbing element in personality will be absent from such writing; but the personal quality of the expression will be all the clearer and more pronounced. What comes out of me, independently of me, must of necessity resemble me. My style is my countenance. A countenance has the general characteristics of the species, but it always has a striking and incommunicable individuality; it is unique in the world and in all the ages; that is, in part, what gives such a fascinating interest to portraits.

Now, our mind is certainly still more original; but we hide it behind general formulas that we have picked up, behind traditional phrases, word combinations that merely represent old habits and not our own ardor of conviction. To show our mind as it is, basing ourselves on acquired habits of expression common to all, but not losing ourselves in them, would be to rouse inexhaustible interest, and it would be art.

The style that suits a mind is like the body that belongs to a soul, or the plant that grows from a particular seed; it has its own proper structure. To imitate is to forego your thought; to write without character is to declare it vague or puerile.

One should never write "in the manner of" so-and-so, even if the so-and-so were oneself. One must not have a manner; truth has none; it is there, objectively real; it is always fresh and new. But truth cannot fail to have an individual ring on each of its instruments.

"All really great men have been original," writes Jules Lachelier;[1] "but they did not aim at it nor think themselves so; on the contrary, it was by trying to make of their words and acts an adequate expression of reason that they found the particular form under which they were destined to express it."

Every instrument has its timbre. If mannerism is an affectation, genuine originality is a manifestation of truth; it intensifies instead of weakening the impression to be produced on the reader, who in his turn will take in what he can, according to his own capacity. What we are proscribing is not the personal feeling which renews and glorifies everything it touches, but self-assertiveness setting itself up against the sway of truth.

Simplicity of style results from these principles. Embellishment is an offense against thought, unless it be an expedient to conceal its void. There are no embellishments in the real; there are only organic necessities. Not that there is no brilliance in nature; but the brilliance itself is organic, it has its rightful existence, it is supported by substructures that never break down.

In nature, the flower is as important a thing as the fruit, and the foliage as the branch; the whole springs from the roots and is but the manifestation of the germ which holds within itself the idea of

[1] A French philosopher, 1832-1918. (Tr. Note.)

the species. Now style, in a good workman's hand, imitates the creations of nature. A sentence, a passage, must be constituted like a living branch, like the fibers of a root, like a tree. Nothing superadded, nothing aside, everything in the direct unbroken curve that goes from germ to germ—from the germ that has come to fruition in the writer to that which is to come to fruition in the reader and to propagate truth or human goodness.

Style is not for its own sake; to attach importance to it on its own account is to misuse and degrade it. How little one must care about truth to let oneself be caught by form, to become a rhymester instead of a poet, a stylist instead of a writer! He who has the necessary talent should carry his style to perfection, which is the right of everything that exists; everyone legitimately wishes to become as expert in writing as an old blacksmith at his iron work; but the blacksmith does not amuse himself twisting his metal into ornamental curves, he makes bars, locks, gates.

Style excludes everything useless; it is strict economy in the midst of riches; it spends whatever is necessary, saves in one place by skillful arrangement, and lavishes its resources elsewhere for the glory of the truth. Its rôle is not to shine, but to set off the matter; it must efface itself, and it is then that its own glory appears. "The beautiful is the removal of all superfluity," said Michelangelo, and Delacroix points out in him "the big settings, the simple cheek lines, the noses broadly drawn." He notes that such a style can only fit in with very firm contours as in Michelangelo, Leonardo, and especially Velasquez; but not in Van Dyck; and that too is a lesson.

Strive to write in the form that is inevitable, given the precise thought or the exact feeling that you have to express. Aim at being understood by all, as is fitting when a man speaks to men, and try to reach whatever in them is directly or indirectly an instrument of truth. "A complete style is that which reaches all souls and all their faculties." [1]

Do not court fashion; your time will of itself influence you and will subordinate itself to the uses of eternity. Give your readers pure spring water, not bitter drugs. Many writers today have a system: every system is a pose, and every pose is an insult to beauty.

Cultivate the art of omission, of elimination, of simplification: that is the secret of strength. The masters end by repeating only that which St. John repeated: "Love one another." The innocent nudity which reveals the splendor of living forms—thought and reality, creations and manifestations of the Word—is the law and the prophets in the matter of style.

Unfortunately this bare purity of the mind is rare; when it does exist it is often allied with empty-headedness. And so only two kinds of mind, the mind of limited power and the mind of genius, seem predisposed to simplicity; the others have to acquire it laboriously, cumbered by their possessions, and unable to limit themselves at their will.

[1] Gratry, *Les Sources.*

II

Style, and speaking more generally, all creative work require detachment. Our obsessing personality must be put aside, the world must be forgotten. When one is thinking of truth, can one allow one's attention to be turned from it by self? What is to be expected of the man who stops short at self? I hope in the man who goes straight forward, beyond his ephemeral personality, towards the immense and the eternal—in the astronomer walking in the company of the stars; in the poet or philosopher or theologian plunged in the study of animate or inanimate matter, of man individual and social, of souls, of angels, and of God. I believe in such a one because the spirit of truth dwells in him, not some wretched preoccupation with self.

We have seen that it is not enough to work with the intelligence alone: the whole man is necessary. But the man who engages in the work must not be the creature of passion, vanity, ambition, or vain desire to please.

Everyone is passionate at times, but passion must at no moment get the upper hand. Everyone is inclined to vanity, but it is a vice if the work itself at bottom is vanity. The important thing is not what we shall get out of knowledge, but what we can give to it. The essential thing is not the reception accorded to our words, but the reception that we ourselves have given to truth, and that we are disposing others to give to it. Of what weight, in view of that sacred purpose, are our petty selfish calculations? Many men who appear to be heartily intent on some work care less for it than for trifling successes. The formation of worlds, the ascent of species, the history of man in society, the economy of labor, serve to get them a purple or red ribbon; their poetry aims at nothing higher than to attract a following of admiring disciples; their pictures aspire to being hung on the line; Corneille once interpreted by Talma[1] turns into a mere pretext for showing off the actor's powers. It is obvious that a mind degenerates when so turned from the subject to itself. Such aims can only degrade work; and even if one is indifferent to immediate success, counting on succeeding later through one's very disinterestedness, the result is the same.

Inspiration is incompatible with selfish desire. Whoever wants something for himself sets truth aside: the jealous God will not sojourn with him. We must work, we said, in a spirit of eternity; what is less eternal than an ambitious aim? You are consecrated to truth, you must serve, not use it.

One throws oneself wholeheartedly only into causes that one would die for. Are you ready to die for the truth? Everything that a real lover of truth writes, everything that he thinks should be like the letters that St. Peter Martyr traced with the blood of his wound as he was dying: *Credo*.

The selfish personality lessens every value that it touches; it contaminates everything, cheapens everything, it disorganizes our powers. The man

[1] A very great French tragic actor, 1763-1826. (Tr. Note.)

who goes ahead, taking his inspiration from truth and leaving the responsibility for consequences to God, that man is a worthy thinker. "For me, to live is Christ," said St. Paul: that was a vocation and a certainty of victorious action. One is not really an intellectual unless one can say: For me, to live is truth.

A form of personality particularly harmful to work is that almost universal hypocrisy which consists in displaying an appearance of knowledge where sincerity would force us to acknowledge ignorance. That he hides intellectual indigence under the cloak of words is the reproach we make to the chance scribbler, the journalist spinning out an article, or the uneducated deputy; but every writer who questions himself honestly will have to admit that he yields every moment, on this point, to the suggestions of pride. One wants to keep one's secret; one hides one's lack of competence; one poses as big, knowing oneself to be little; one "asserts," "declares," "is sure"; at bottom one does not know; one imposes on the public; and, half-duped by one's own game, one deceives oneself.

Another fundamental fault is to affect in our thought that pseudo-originality that a moment ago we condemned in style. It is intolerable pride to try to force truth into our personal mold, and it ends in stupidity. Truth is essentially impersonal. When it borrows our voice and our mind it will take the color of our personality without any effort of ours: it will do this all the more that we are not thinking about ourselves: but to exert pressure on truth so as to make it resemble us is to warp it—is to violate immortal reality by substituting for it our ephemeral self.

"Do not look to see whence truth comes," said St. Thomas: neither look to see on whom it reflects glory; be desirous that your reader, with your work before him, does not for his part look to see whence the truth comes. This lofty disinterestedness is the mark of a great soul; to strive for it, to make it a law always acknowledged —even if not always obeyed—is to correct our poor nature which cannot be entirely delivered from its weakness. One grows in that way with the only true greatness. The humble candlestick has its share of glory when truth, the authentic living flame, shines from the candle of the mind.

You must also, I said, forget the public. "The farther away from the reader a book is written the more powerful it is," said Père Gratry in *Les Sources,* and he gives as examples Pascal's *Thoughts,* Bossuet's writings for the Dauphin, above all the *Summa* of St. Thomas of Aquin; a comparison between the *Petit Carême*[1] and the *Discours synodaux* of Massillon confirms the statement. It is true and Vauvenargues[2] agrees when

[1] *Petit Carême,* Lenten sermons preached before the court. In them, says Gratry, the preacher "really goes too far in drawing out his thought: the web is so delicate as to weary the eye"; while the Synodal Addresses, "almost improvised for a few country priests in Auvergne," are "living energetic pages." (Tr. Note.)

[2] A well known French moralist, author of a book entitled *Maximes* (1746). (Tr. Note.)

he says: "Everything that one has thought out only for others usually lacks naturalness."

But that does not mean that one may neglect the neighbor and take no account of being useful to one's fellows. The intellectual belongs to everyone and should know it. But to be concerned to serve is not to take one's cue from current opinion. We must not allow ourselves to be influenced by fear of what people will say; we must beware of yielding to the pressure of a spirit of cowardly conformity which proclaims itself everybody's friend in the hope that everybody will obligingly return the compliment.

To look for public approval is to deprive the public of a force that it counted on. Are you not devoted to your fellows? Have they not the right to ask you: where is your work? Now thought will not be your own work if anxiety to please and to adapt yourself to others enslaves your pen. The public will then be thinking for you whose duty it was to think for it.

Seek the approval of God; be intent only on truth, for yourself and others; do not be a slave; make yourself worthy to say with Paul: "The word of God is not bound."

This virtue of independence is so much the more necessary as the public, in the mass, has all the qualities needed to pull you down. The public has the elementary school mentality. In most circles and by the majority of its votes it proclaims conventions, not truths; it likes to be flattered; it fears above everything to have its quietude disturbed.

To get it to listen to the essential truths, you must impose them by sheer insistence. You can do it, and the solitary thinker must try to exercise this felicitous violence.

The thinker's power to succeed in this comes from taking his stand on his own thought and on the nature of things, from "striking like a deaf man" as Madame de Sévigné said of Bourdaloue, and from shouting out the danger-cry which ends by rousing and subduing souls.

The only really powerful and really compelling force is strong conviction joined to a character which offers guarantees to poor humanity. The very people who require you to court their favor despise a flatterer and surrender to a master. If you are of this world, this world will love you because you are its own; but its silent disdain will be the measure of your fall.

This perverse world loves, at bottom, only saints; this cowardly world dreams of heroes; Roger Bontemps [1] grows grave and has thoughts of conversion when he sees an ascetic. In such a world you must not yield to public opinion and write as if humanity were looking over your shoulder. You must shake yourself free of other people, as well as of yourself. In the intellectual domain as in every other, to rise above man is to prepare wondrous things, for it is opening the way to the Spirit.

Seated at your writing table and in the solitude in which God speaks to the heart, you should listen

[1] An easy-living, happy-go-lucky person: the surname of an old French poet popularized by Béranger. (Tr. Note.)

as a child listens and write as a child speaks. The child is simple and detached because he has as yet no self-will, no pre-established positions, no artificial desires, no passions. His naïve confidence and direct speech have an immense interest for us. A mature man, enriched by experience, who should yet preserve this simplicity of the child would be an admirable repository of truth, and his voice would reecho in the souls of his fellow men.

III

Creative work calls for other virtues also; its demands are on a level with its worth. I speak here together of three of these requirements, which subserve one another and insure results that are not poor or inadequate. You must bring to your work constancy which keeps steadily at the task; patience which bears difficulties well; perseverance which prevents the will from flagging.

"You must not imagine," says Nicole, "that the life of study is an easy life. . . . The reason is that there is nothing more against nature than uniformity and stillness, because nothing gives us more occasion to be alone with ourselves. Change and external occupations take us out of ourselves and distract us by making us forget ourselves. Moreover, this medium of words has always something dead about it, it has nothing that piques our self-love or rouses our passions strongly.[1] It is de-

[1] Nicole, a 17th century moralist, was thinking of the carefully chastened and clarified language of "classical" French. (Tr. Note.)

void of action and movement. . . . It speaks little to us of ourselves and gives us little ground for contemplating ourselves with pleasure. It affords little encouragement to our hopes; and all this tends strangely to mortify our self-love, which, being unsatisfied, causes us weariness and distaste in everything that we do."[1] This analysis, which recalls Pascal's theory of diversion,[2] might take us far. I merely pick out the fact that as "weariness and distaste" are in our case formidable enemies, we must plan to overcome them.

Everyone knows those intellectuals who work spasmodically, in fits interrupted by spells of laziness and indifference. There are rents in the fabric of their destiny: they make of it a tattered garment roughly drawn together, instead of a noble drapery. We, on the contrary, mean to be intellectuals all the time, and we intend others to recognize the fact. People will know what we are by our way of resting, of idling, of tying our shoes: still more will it be evident in our fidelity to work, in our prompt and regular return to our task, and in its continuity.

When Edison was asked one day to say to a

[1] Nicole *op. cit.*, page 255.

[2] *Divertissement:* literally, the word means *turning aside* from ourselves and our destiny to find distraction in occupations, amusements, etc. "The whole calamity of man" (wrote Pascal) "comes from one single thing, that he cannot keep quiet in a room." That is the cause of all our misfortunes; and if we look for the reason of this restlessness we shall find that there is an effectual one, the craving to evade the vision of our destiny. (Tr. Note, taken from Jacques Chevalier.)

child something that he might remember, the great inventor uttered with a smile the words: "My boy, don't keep your eye on the clock." Edison himself was so little in the habit of watching the clock that on the day of his marriage—a love-match—he had to be sent for; he had got lost in one of his investigations.

It is a glorious thing to be wholly engaged in what one is doing, like God, who is not separate from His work. But if an occupation is beneath one's personality, one might as well put nothing of oneself into it.

One is often tempted to lose time because "it's not worthwhile settling down," because " it's just on the hour." We forget that these odds and ends of time, which indeed do not lend themselves to anything serious, are just the moments for preparing the work or touching it up, for verifying references, looking up notes, sorting papers, etc. That would be so much out of the way for the hours of really serious application, and the moments so turned to account would be as useful as the others, because these secondary tasks belong to the work and are indispensable to it.

Even during real working hours, there is a temptation to interrupt our effort as soon as the slightest happening brings back the "weariness" and rouses the "distaste" of which Nicole spoke. The ruses of sloth are endless, like those of children. Looking for a word that will not come, one begins to sketch something on the margin of the paper and the drawing must be finished. Opening the dictionary, one is attracted by some curious word, then by another, and there one stays, tangled in a thicket. Your eyes fall on some object: you go to put it in its place, and you find yourself led on to waste a quarter of an hour on a trifle. Someone passes by: there is a friend in the next room: you think of a telephone call, or the newspaper comes, you glance at it, and you are soon lost in it. It may be even that one idea brings another in its train and that the work itself prevents you from working; some thought sets you dreaming and carries you away along the vistas of imagination.

In inspired moments these snares are less to be feared: the joy of discovery or of creation carries you along: but bad hours always come, and while they last, temptation is very strong. Sometimes it takes real strength of soul to get over these small difficulties. All workers bewail the moments of depression that break in on the hours of ardor and threaten to bring their results to nothing. When the disgust with work lasts long, one feels that one would rather plant cabbages than pursue a wearisome study; one envies the laborer who on his side calls you a good-for-nothing because you sit quietly in your chair. What danger there is of giving up when you are in this distressing state of mind!

It is most of all at turning-points in our study that we must look out for sudden or insidious attacks of this kind. In every work there are troublesome transitions; to make one part follow closely on another is the great difficulty in study and creation. Everything depends on the connection of ideas. One is moving forward in a straight line, and there comes a bend of which it is hard to measure the angle; one does not sense the new direction; one hesitates, and it is then that the demon of laziness comes on the scene.

Sometimes it is good to stop for a while, when one does not see the right succession of ideas and is exposed to the grave danger of making artificial transitions. It may be that later on light will come without any seeking. I said that there are graces of the night, of the bright morning, of moments of effortless musing. But to break off for a while is not laziness. Take up some other side of the work and transfer your keen application to that.

Reject vigorously every unjustified interruption. If you are too tired, make a deliberate pause so as to pull yourself together. Nervous exhaustion would lead you nowhere. Possible remedies for fatigue are, for example, reading a few pages of a favorite author, reciting something aloud, kneeling down and saying a prayer so as to modify the state of the organism and therefore more or less refresh the mind, a few rhythmical movements or breathing exercises in the open air. Then get back to your effort.

Some people have recourse to stimulants; but that is a fatal method. The effect is only momentary; it grows less with use; the quantity has to be increased daily; and the progression ends in physical and mental degeneracy.

Walking, whether in the open air or in one's

study, is a more harmless stimulant. Many workers thus set their brain in motion by means of the motion of their limbs. "My foot is a writer too," said Nietzsche.

But your most normal stimulant is courage. Courage is sustained, not only by prayer, but by calling up anew the vision of the goal. The prisoner who wants to escape from prison contrives to develop every kind of energy; he does not weary of remote preparations, or of resuming them after a setback: liberty is calling him. Have you not to escape from error, to win the liberty of the mind in a finished work? Keep your eyes on its completion and that vision will give you fresh courage.

Another effect of constancy is to overcome those impressions of imaginary weariness which affect the mind as well as the body. At the beginning of a walking excursion, it often happens that the first steep ascent finds you inert and breathless; your limbs ache; you are almost inclined to give up and go home. But if you keep on, the joints grow supple, the muscles act freely, the chest expands and you feel the delight of activity. It is the same with study. You must not yield to the first sense of fatigue; you must push on; you must force the inner energy to reveal itself. Little by little the mechanism gets into play, you adapt yourself, and a period of enthusiasm may follow on the first painful inertia.

Whatever be the cause of your difficulties you must go through them without flinching, keeping your self-mastery. Each spell of work is like a racecourse with a certain number of obstacles. You jump a hedge; a little farther on you come to a ditch, then a bank, and so on. You do not stop at the first hurdle, you jump it; and between the obstacles there are quiet stretches where you go ahead at a good pace. One difficulty overcome shows you how to overcome others; one effort spares you three or four; a minute's courage carries you through a day and the hard work ends by being fruitful and joyous.

In your life as a whole this tenacity will help to make your activity easier and easier. One acquires facility in thinking just as one acquires facility in playing the piano, in riding, or painting: St. Thomas used to dictate in his sleep. The mind gets into the way of doing what is often demanded of it. Even if you have no memory, you acquire memory for the subject always before your mind; if you are inclined to be scatterbrained, you attain the degree of attention of a professional; if you have little aptitude for distinguishing ideas, your judgment grows keener and surer by persevering contact with great thinkers. In every subject-matter, after a certain number of efforts to start, your motor warms up, and the road flies past.

Amiel one day asked himself in his Journal: "Why are you weak? Because times without number you have given in. So you have become the plaything of circumstances. It is you who have made them strong, not they who have made you weak."

Learn constancy by persistent application and by

obstinately returning to the interrupted study: a day will come when the recurring fits of weariness will vanish, when moments of distaste will have little effect; you will have become a man; the inconstant worker is a mere child.

Experience shows that many difficulties are overcome in advance by the man who throws himself energetically into his work, like a runner starting off with a bound. Still, there will always remain a considerable number that must be gotten over by a virtue akin to constancy, patience.

Great thinkers have all complained of the tribulations of the life of thought, declaring that their labors, although for them a necessity and a condition of happiness, caused them long-drawn-out torment, sometimes even real agony.

The laws of the brain are obscure; its workings depend but little on the will; when it refuses its service, what is to be done? When the threads of knowledge grow tangled and the hours go by in vain, when a painful feeling of powerlessness takes hold of you and there is not the least sign that this trial will soon end, where are you to turn and what help can you call on but the help of God?

When you succeed your reader will think it all quite simple; he will criticize your weaknesses without mercy; he will not suspect the cost of the work. But indeed he must not be allowed to suspect it. "Creations realized at the price of a great deal of work," said Michelangelo, "must in spite of the truth appear easy and effortless. . . . The great rule is to take much trouble to produce things that seem to have cost none." Did not Boileau somewhat similarly boast that he had taught Racine the art of making easy verses with difficulty? In the domain of science, Biot said: "There is nothing so easy as what was discovered yesterday, nor so difficult as what will be discovered tomorrow." But the public does not suspect this. You must carry your burden alone, and great men warn you that this burden of thought is the heaviest that man can carry.

In research, you must be as indomitable as the polar or Central African explorer. In attacking or resisting error, you will need the endurance and ardor of Caesar or of Wellington. Work requires heroism just as a battle does. One's study is sometimes a trench where one has to stand firm, like a good martyr.

When you feel yourself defenseless, overcome; when the road stretches out before you interminably, or when, having no doubt mistaken your direction, you have the impression of being lost, completely astray, wrapped in a thick fog, then is the time to draw on stores of energy held in reserve. Persist, stand up to the difficulty, be patient in the great sense of the word, which calls up the Passion of the Master. Ardor is easier than patience but both are necessary and success is the reward of their combination.

To the alpinist walking through a cloud it seems as if the universe were plunged in night; he goes on and he finds the sunlight beyond. In a closed room in bad weather, the elements outside seem impossible to face; you go out, you make your way quietly and fine weather comes back.

It is principally the length of time required that makes the art of thinking so forbidding and so out of proportion to the degree of courage that people ordinarily possess. *Ars longa, vita brevis.* There is plenty of scope here for the virtue of patience. By respecting the laws of birth and development, and by not insulting knowledge through ill-judged hurry, you will gain more than by a headlong rush. Truth and nature proceed at an even pace, and nature operates through periods of duration in comparison with which the life and death of our globe are a mere sunrise and sunset.

"What goes on in the depths of the springs," writes Nietzsche, "goes on slowly; one must wait long to find out what has fallen into their depths." [1] The soul is that secret spring: do not try prematurely to clear up its mystery. The stores of time belong to God; little by little He doles them out to us; but it is not our part to demand them or to grow impatient. Nothing is precious but what comes at the right moment.

Avoid the fuss and flurry of the man who is pressed for time. Hasten slowly. In the realm of mind, quietness is better than speed. There more than elsewhere the proverb is verified: All things come to him who waits. "A well-filled life is long," said Leonardo da Vinci. To the man who takes his time belongs all duration, itself situate in eternity. Work then in a spirit of eternity. Do not confuse

[1] Friedrich Nietzsche, *So sprach Zarathustra.*

the impetus of a noble enthusiasm with the exciting stimuli which are almost its opposite, for they break its rhythm. The ordering of ideas and the delicate elaboration of new thoughts is a work needing peace; you cannot accomplish it in a state of disturbance. Do you want to lose time through the foolish fear of not having enough?

As a Christian, you must respect God in His providence. It is He who lays down the conditions of knowledge: impatience is a revolt against Him. When feverish excitement takes hold of you, spiritual slavery is close at hand, interior liberty vanishes. It is not now you yourself who act, still less Christ in you. You are no longer doing the work of the Word.

Why press on immoderately, when the road itself is a goal, the means an end? When one looks at Niagara, does one long to see it hurry? Intellectual activity has its own worth at every stage. Effort is a virtue and a conquest. He who works for God and as God wills abides in God. What does it matter if time runs on, when one is established in God?

The consummation of steady constancy and patience is perseverance, which completes the work. "He that shall persevere unto the end, he shall be saved," says the Gospel. Intellectual salvation has no other law. "No man putting his hand to the plow and looking back" is worthy, in the intellectual order either, of the kingdom of heaven.

How many workers have given up plowing and sowing, and foregone the harvest! The whole world is peopled with these deserters. In the pursuit of knowledge the first experiments have the character of eliminatory tests; one after another the weak characters give up, the valiant hold out; at the end there are left only the three hundred of Gideon, or the thirty of David.

To persevere is to will; he who does not persevere does not will, he only plans. He who lets go has never really held; he who ceases to love has never loved. Our destiny is one; a work which is a part of it is still more necessarily one. The true intellectual is by definition a man who perseveres. He takes on himself the task of learning and teaching; he loves truth with his whole being; he is consecrated to his work; he does not give it up prematurely.

Great lives have all displayed this supreme mark of superiority. They end like a glorious day. The red light of the setting sun is no less beautiful than the first golden gleams of morning and it has grandeur in addition. The man of character who has worked unfailingly throughout a long life can go down like the sun into a quiet and splendid death; his work follows him, and at the same time remains to us.

You who walk in the footsteps of the great, be not of the number of those cowardly wayfarers who desert—who go a stage, stop, lose the way, sit down as if exhausted and go back sooner or later to the trodden places. You must hold out to the end of the journey. "Fair and softly goes far in a day," and a few great strides without perseverance are mere useless movements leading nowhere.

Strengthen your will and entrust it to the Lord so that He may set His seal on it. To will is to be subject, to be enchained. The necessity imposed by duty, or by a deliberate resolution even though it carry no obligation, must be as compelling for us as the necessities imposed by nature. Is not a moral bond more than a material bond.

Learn then, after having decided on your task, to stick to it with resourceful inflexibility; shut out even lesser duties, and still more, of course, all infidelity to your undertaking. Strive to deepen your work, so as to force duration into your service in that one of its dimensions that is directly accessible to you. Carried along on its stream, you will take advantage of it until it fails you. You will be of the line of faithful thinkers. The giants of work, such men as Aristotle, Augustine, Albert the Great, Thomas of Aquin, Leibnitz, Littré, Pasteur, will acknowledge you for their son; and you will go worthily to meet Him who is patiently waiting for you.

IV

If the requirements of these three virtues are satisfied there is little fear that the result will be mediocre or imperfect. However it is a good thing to insist strongly on the necessity of perfecting, and on the duty of bringing to completion, whatever one has thought well of undertaking.

One must surely have reflected before starting on a piece of work. Only a scatterbrain rushes into an adventure, little or big, without having, as the Gospel says, "counted the cost." Wisdom demands that one should face the obligation of finishing a thing when one is deliberating on the fitness of beginning it. Not to complete a work is to destroy it. "He that is loose and slack in his work is the brother of him that wasteth his own works," says Proverbs (18:9).

What is the use of a half-built house? What does it tell us about the man who laid the foundations and the lower courses? Such a ruin suggests some calamity; it is unthinkable that a living man or one whom misfortune has spared should endure these walls which are like the broken columns in cemeteries. And do you, a builder in the spirit, want to make of your past a field of debris?

There are some people on whom one can count; when they promise they keep their word. Now every beginning is a promise, unless it is a piece of folly. Others give their word, swear by all they hold sacred, and nothing happens; you would think that they have some natural inaptitude for undertaking an obligation; you cannot bind them and they cannot bind themselves; they are like running water.

People like that represent a morally inferior species; the intellectual who resembles them is not really an intellectual, his vocation has condemned itself. You who have the sacred call, make up your mind to be faithful. There is a law within you, let it be obeyed. You have said: "I will do this," do it.

A case of conscience is before you: settle it to your honor; every unfinished work would be a reproach to you.

I see a cause of moral decadence in abandoning a project or an undertaking. One grows used to giving-up; one resigns oneself to disorder, to an uncomfortable conscience; one gets a habit of shilly-shallying. Thence comes a loss of dignity that can have no favorable effect on one's progress.

Measure your cloth ten times; cut out once; tack carefully, and when the time comes to do the sewing, let nothing on earth make you say: I give it up.

The consequence will be that the sewing, as far as in you lies, will be perfect. *Finished* means ended, but it also means perfect, and these two senses reinforce each other. I do not really finish that in which I refuse to aim at the best. What is not perfected *is* not. According to Spinoza, being and perfection correspond to the same idea; being and good are convertible.

It is related of Titian that he sketched his pictures boldly, worked them up to a certain point and then put the painting against the wall until it had become like a stranger to him. Then he took it up again, and viewing it with a "hostile eye," he obliged it to turn into a masterpiece.

When you have roughed out a piece of work, you must put it aside like that, rest your eyes and look at it from a proper distance. If you do not approve of it then, start afresh. If it comes up to your level, critize it minutely, in every detail, and come back and back to the task until you can say: my capacity is exhausted; whatever deficiencies remain, may God and my neighbor forgive me. *"Quod potui feci; veniam da mihi, posteritas,"* said Leonardo da Vinci in his epitaph.

It is not necessary that you should compose a lengthy work. If what you do corresponds to your talent, to the graces granted and the time accorded you; if you have put your whole self into it, and if the will of Providence is satisfied in you by entire obedience, all is well. You will always do much, if you accomplish perfectly what you do. Something that you might do badly could add nothing to the work and would even take from it, like a stain on a precious piece of silk.

An intellectual vocation is no half-and-half thing; you must give yourself to it entirely. Your life, which as a whole is sacred to the God of Truth, is His in every separate occurrence of which it is made up. In each work say to yourself: it is my duty to do it, and therefore to do it well, since what is not finished *is* not. In as far as I do it badly, I am missing my life, disobeying the Lord, and failing my brethren. In so far, I am unfaithful to my vocation. To have a vocation is to be obliged to perfection.

An important bit of practical advice is in place here. When you have decided on a work, when you have clearly conceived and carefully prepared it, and are actually beginning: settle *immediately* by a vigorous effort the quality that it is to have. Do not count on going back over it. When laziness whispers: "Go ahead anyhow now, you will come back to this later," say to yourself that this idea of going back on what one has done is nearly always an illusion. When you have once gone down the slope, you will hardly climb up again. You will not find the courage to rethink *ab ovo* a mediocre piece of work; your cowardice today is a poor guarantee for your heroism tomorrow. As for the corrections you might make, even though they were perfect in themselves, they would be out of tone. A work should be fundamentally of one piece. Beethoven remarked that a passage introduced as an afterthought never quite fits in. A fine work is like a flow of lava. Titian went thoroughly over his picture, but, keeping the original note, purely and simply with a view to perfecting it; he changed nothing in the idea, the composition, the fundamental lines. The effort had already been made: he was only consummating it.

Therefore put out your very best at the moment of creation. When you have brought forth the work, you will treat it like the child that one feeds and educates, but whose heredity is fixed, whose fundamental characteristics are established. That will be the moment to apply to the offspring of your spirit the saying of the Bible: "He that spareth the rod hateth his son." (Prov. 13:24.)

V

All this severity with ourselves presupposes that the work undertaken is suited to us and proportioned to our resources. If the prey is more powerful than the hunter, it devours him. For such a case it is absurd to lay down rules. You cannot give directions for attacking leopards to a man who courses hares.

The last of the *Sixteen Precepts* of St. Thomas is this: "*Altiora te ne quaesieris,* do not seek things above you." That is great wisdom. The ancient oracle had already said: "Do not force your destiny; do not try to go beyond the duty imposed on you." Intellectual work is but the prolongation of our inborn tendencies. We exist, we act, the work comes to birth: that is the series. If you try to add iron to lead, silk to cotton, they will not hold together, no good will come of it. Vocation uses our resources, but does not create them. The poorly gifted intellectual will never be other than a failure: but to be poorly gifted may be relative to a particular work. And that is the point we now desire to make.

Try to discern in every occurrence the effort that befits you, the discipline you are capable of, the sacrifice you can make, the subject you can deal with, the thesis you can write, the book that you can read with profit, the public you can serve. Take the measure of all these things with humility and confidence. If need be, ask for advice, but do not forget that irresponsibility and indifference are widespread amongst advisers. Make up your mind to the best of your ability. Then throw yourself with your whole heart into your task.

Every work is great when it is in exact measure. A work that exceeds its proper limits is the least of all. We have said repeatedly that your work, your proper work, is unique; another man's work is equally so, do not interchange with him. You alone can do well what is laid upon you; you would do badly what your neighbor will do well. God is satisfied in all.

To proportion one's task to one's powers, to undertake to speak only when one knows, not to force oneself to think what one does not think, or to understand what one does not understand—to avoid the danger of missing the substance of things and disguising its absence under big words: all that is great wisdom. Pride rebels against it; but pride is the enemy of the mind as it is of the conscience. A presumptuous man is overwhelmed by his work, covers himself with ridicule, and brings his real strength to nothing. Breaking faith with himself, he breaks faith with the world; he is a flame that has gone out.

Success in every order is always attained on the same conditions: to reflect at the start, to begin at the beginning, to proceed methodically, to advance slowly, to give out all one's strength. But the first object of initial reflection is to decide what we are fit for. The "Know thyself" of Socrates is not only the key to morality, but to every vocation, since to be called to something is to see our individual path marked out along the wide human road.

chapter 9

The Worker and the Man

I

After having made so many demands on the intellectual and apparently forged so many chains for him, will it seem like irony to turn to him once more and say: Keep your soul free. What matters most in life is not knowledge, but character; and character would be endangered if a man were under his work, so to speak, struggling with Sisyphus' stone. There is a knowledge other than that which is of the domain of memory: the knowledge of how to live. Study must be an act of life, must serve life, must feel itself impregnated with life. Of the two kinds of men, those who endeavor to know something, and those who try to be someone, the palm is to the second. What we know is like a beginning, a rough sketch only; the man is the finished work.

It is certainly true that intellectuality contributes to the sovereignty of man; but it is not enough. Besides morality, which includes the life of religion, various broad aspects of the human condition must be considered. We have spoken of life in society, of practical activities: let us add communion with nature, care of one's home, the arts, friendly and formal gatherings, a little poetry, the practice of speaking, intelligent sport, public demonstrations.

It is hard to settle exactly the measure of all these things; I have confidence that the reader will find here at least the spirit in which to decide. It is a sure indication both for thought and practice to be able to appreciate the relative value of things.

Study is intended to bring about the extension of our being: it must not end by making us narrow. If art is man added to nature, knowledge is nature added to man: in both cases we must safeguard the man.

Pascal refuses his esteem to the specialist who is only a specialist; he does not want a man's book to be remembered the moment he comes into a room. "It is a bad mark," he says, and he does not mean it only from the point of view of comparative study which we have advocated; he is thinking of a harmonious human whole.

We must always be more than we are; the philosopher must be something of a poet, the poet something of a philosopher; the craftsman must be poet and philosopher on occasion, and the people recognize this fact. The writer must be a practical man, and the practical man must know how to write. Every specialist is first of all a person, and the essential quality of the person is beyond anything that he thinks or does.

Our destiny cannot be taken in as we take in some particular thing: we open out to it "with the flower of the mind" as Zoroaster says. Particular aims have not the value of life itself, nor acts that of action, nor talent that of a wide intuition in which the whole of existence finds a place; the work has not the value of the workman. Everything is harmful when severed from its broad connections, and only in our total setting does our soul reach its full expansion.

The man who thinks exclusively of his work, works badly: he cramps himself; he acquires a specialized bent which becomes a defect. The mind must stay open, must keep contact with humanity and with the world, so that every time it comes back to its work, it brings capacity for a new flight.

We have already quoted this saying of a rabbi: "Into a bushel full of nuts one can pour in addition many measures of oil"; wc then applied it to studies which help one another instead of being in conflict. By the nuts let us now understand specialized work; one can add to it the oil of effortless intellectual life, leisure nobly employed, nature, art; all this does not overload the mind but, on the contrary, eases its strain.

The specialized work itself will be the gainer. It gains richly from society, friendships, external action: I have explained why. Here I am only expanding the conclusions we have reached, for they have a general bearing. Do you imagine that any specialized pursuit whatever is out of keeping with a visit to the Louvre, an evening spent listening to the Eroica Symphony or the Oedipus Rex, a walk about Versailles under the autumn trees, the sight of a sunset, a patriotic gathering in the great amphitheater of the Sorbonne, the Olympic Games, a Mystery play at Jumièges or in the theatre of Orange, a great sermon at Notre Dame?

It would be a very poor conception of thought not to see how it is connected with every manifestation of creative power.

Nature renews everything, refreshes every well-formed mind, opens up new vistas and suggests surveys that abstract thinking knows nothing of. The tree is a teacher; the field teems with ideas as with anemones or daisies; the clouds and stars in the revolving sky bring fresh inspiration; the mountains steady our thoughts with their mass; and the course of the running streams starts the mind on lofty meditations.

I know a man who at the sight of a rapid mountain torrent inevitably thought of the movement of worlds—those masses that rush through space with the same speed, under the governance of the same laws, depending on the same forces, thanks to the same God with whom everything begins and to whom everything returns. Going back to his work he felt himself uplifted by the unique Force, filled with the Presence that is everywhere; and his obscure activity was rooted in communion with all being.

Yet you let your mind get cramped and your

heart grow dry, and you imagine that it is loss of time to follow the course of the torrents or to wander among the stars. The universe fills man with its glory, and you do not know it. The star of evening set against the darkening sky is lonely, it wants a place in your thought, and you refuse to admit it. You write, you compute, you string propositions together, you elaborate your theses, and you do not *look*.

Who does not know that in listening to music an intellectual may get an impression of greatness, beauty, power which is immediately transposed into his ordinary modes of thinking, furthers his purposes, colors his customary themes, and will presently enrich his working time? Does he not jot down rapidly on the back of his program the plan of a chapter or of a treatise, the idea of a development, or a vivid image? The harmony has heightened the tone of his inspiration, and the rhythm in which he is caught up like a passerby in a troop of soldiers on the march, has carried him away on new paths.

At Saint Sulpice, painting the Chapel of the Angels, Delacroix revelled in the sound of the great organ and in the chanting; to that harmony he attributed the extraordinary success of his Jacob wrestling, and of the rider in the *Heliodorus*.

Music has this precious quality for the intellectual that as it conveys no precise ideas, it interferes with none. It awakens states of soul, from which each one in his particular task will draw what he wills. Rodin makes a statue of it, Corot a landscape, Gratry a burning page, Pasteur a more inspired and attentive spell of research. Everything is contained in harmony, and everything is regenerated by it. Rhythm, the father of the world, is also the father of the intellect in which the world is reflected. On the indistinct horizon of his reverie, each one sees the vision of his choice and records its features in his own speech.

According to St. Thomas, the circumstances of our personality and surroundings form part of our activities; they concur in making of these an integral whole on which they stamp their characteristics. Shall the act of thinking be the only exception? Will our thought not be influenced by the setting—imaginative, sensorial, spiritual, social—that we succeed in providing, so that it may not now be an isolated song, but a voice in the orchestra?

One is a poor thing all by oneself in one's study! It is true one can bring the universe into it and people it with God; but that divine inhabitation is effective only after long experience, of which the elements are everywhere about us. Should I write under the impression of nature and of universal beauty, if great scenery, the peaceful countryside, the vision of the achievements of art, had not previously educated me?

We must widen our work in that way, in order not to be like the chained galley slave, or to turn intellectuality into an instrument of torture. Work is a free act.

You, therefore, who intend to devote yourself to

the vocation of study, beware of turning your back for its sake on the rest of life. Give up nothing of what belongs to man. Preserve a balance in which the dominant weight does not try to carry all the rest with it. Learn to defend a thesis and to look at a sunrise, to bury yourself in profound abstractions and to play, like the Divine Master, with children. Nowadays the pedants' gowns and pointed caps that Pascal mocked at are not worn; but they still exist, they are hidden within, they are in the soul: do not array yourself in them. Refuse to be a brain detached from its body, and a human being who has cut out his soul. Do not make a monomania of work.

The intellectual I have in view is a man of wide and varied knowledge complementary to a special study thoroughly pursued; he loves the arts and natural beauty; his mind shows itself to be one in everyday occupations and in meditation: he is the same man in the presence of God, of his fellows, and of his maid, carrying within him a world of ideas and feelings that are not only written down in books and in discourses, but flow into his conversation with his friends, and guide his life.

At bottom, everything is connected and everything is the same thing. Intellectuality admits of no compartments. All the objects of our thought are so many doors into the "secret garden," the "wine cellar" which is the goal of ardent research. Thoughts and activities, realities and their reflections, all have one and the same Father. Philosophy, art, travel, domestic cares, finance, poetry, and tennis can be allied with one another, and conflict only through lack of harmony.

What is necessary every moment is to be where we ought to be and to do the thing that matters. Everything makes one harmony in the concert of the human and the divine.

II

Everyone can see that to cultivate the kind of breadth we advocate is in itself to relax. The better part of relaxation is contained in the secondary modes of life that we have mentioned. It is a good thing however to speak more explicitly about rest, which is the pendant of work; through which therefore work is in a certain way defined, showing itself excessive, or reasonable, subject or not subject to the human rule which is confirmed by the law of God.

Nothing must be in excess. Work, precisely because it is a duty, requires limits which maintain it in full vigor, make it lasting, and enable it to yield in the course of life the greatest total effect of which it is capable.

Intemperance is a sin because it destroys us; and we have the obligation to use life wisely because we have the obligation to live. Now it is not only in coarse enjoyments that we can fall into intemperance; the subtlest and the noblest delights can partake of its harmful character. To love truth at the expense of prudence—that is, at the expense of the truth of life—is an absurdity. It proves that in spite of our protestations it is not truth that we love, but the pleasure we take in it, like those lovers of whom it is said that they like to love, and that they love love rather than its object.

Relaxation is a duty, like hygiene in which it is included, like the conservation of energy. "I pray thee, spare thyself at times," said St. Augustine to his disciple.[1] The mind of itself does not grow tired, but the mind in the body grows tired; our powers of thought are proportioned to a certain element of action. Moreover, since the world of sense is our connatural setting, and since all the little practical actions form the web of the life we are adapted for, one cannot leave that lower sphere and rise up to the abstract without some fatigue. The effort cannot be continuous. We must come back to nature and plunge into it in order to recover our energy.[2]

The man engaged in contemplation is "heavier than air": he can keep aloft only by a considerable expenditure of force: in a short time the supply of gas is exhausted and he must "fill up" again.

We can accept without paradox this saying of Bacon, which the discoveries of physiology corroborate: "To spend too much Time in Studies is Sloth." It is sloth directly, in as much as it is incapacity to overcome a fixed habit, to put on the brake sometimes. It is sloth indirectly because to refuse to rest is implicitly to refuse an effort that rest would render possible, and that overwork will

[1] *De Musica,* c. II.

[2] Cf. St. Thomas, 2a 2ae, qu. 168, art. 2.

make problematical. But it is sloth in a more hidden fashion also. In fact, physiologically, rest is tremendous work. When mental activity is interrupted, the inner nature of the body enters on a process of restoration which should be thorough. What we call leisure is but a transformation of energy.

In a theater, when the curtain falls, a whole army of workmen hurries on to the stage, cleaning, repairing, altering, and so preparing for the next act. If a stage manager were to interrupt or hinder this work, would he not be an enemy of the play, of the author, the interpreters, the public, himself? Similarly the man who overworks himself is going against his own vocation, against Him who has called him to it, against his brethren who would profit by what he does, against his own good.

The best way of all to relax would be, if possible, not to get tired; I mean, so to balance one's work that one operation would afford rest from another. In medicine, the effects of a harmful drug are often counteracted by its opposite. Not everything causes the same kind of fatigue, nor at the same moment. The puddler perspiring at his furnace would find it a rest to stack hay in the open country, and the man who stacks the hay to distribute it in the mangers.

We have already made some suggestions on this point. In speaking of the use of time, and then apropos of constancy in work, we touched on the principle of dividing up one's tasks. Not everything in intellectual work involves exhausting concentration; there are preliminaries, asides, practical corollaries of thought and creation. Choosing books, sorting papers, gathering up notes, classifying manuscripts, pasting insets in your margins, correcting proofs, tidying your study and your books; all these things keep you occupied but are not work. By good organization it is possible to work intensively only when one is deliberately ready to do so, and in the intervals to get through many of these not very tiring tasks, which yet are indispensable, and therefore have of themselves a certain value of contemplation.

This plan of arranging one's tasks according to the demands they make on the brain will have a double advantage: it will prevent overstrain, and will restore its pure value to intensive work. When one does not make room for rest, the rest one does not take takes itself: it steals into the work, under the form of distractions, of sleepiness, of necessary things that demand attention, not having been foreseen at the right time.

I am in the full swing of creative effort: I lack a reference; there is no ink in the bottle; I have forgotten to sort my notes; a book, a manuscript that I want are in another room, or buried under a pile from which they must be dug out. An hour ago all that would have been done easily, joyously, looking forward to the quiet hour that I was getting ready for. Now it disturbs me; my creative impulse dies. If I omitted these preparations because of some nominal work, some inferior occupation that I was bent on through lack of self-control, there is a double disaster; I arrive at this result: no real rest, no real work. Disorder reigns.

Avoid carefully, I said, in regard to the "moments of plenitude" the half-work which is half-rest and which is no good for anything. Work energetically, then relax, even if it is only that relative relaxation which prepares, subserves, or concludes the work.

Complete rest will, however, also be necessary, complete, I mean, through momentarily giving up every preoccupation with one's task—except that of the "permanent work" that we have seen to be so easy and so profitable.

St. Thomas explains that the true rest of the soul is joy, some activity in which we delight. Games, familiar conversation, friendship, family life, pleasant reading such as we have spoken of, communion with nature, some art accessible to us, some not tiring manual work, an intelligent stroll about town, theatrical performances that are not too exacting or too exciting, sport in moderation; these are our means of relaxation.

But they must not be carried to excess either. Protracted relaxation, besides eating up time, interfers with the momentum of a life of work. It is very important for each person to discover the harmonious alternation which leaves this momentum at its maximum with the minimum of fatigue. To work too long is to get worn-out; to stop too soon is to fail in giving one's measure. In the same way, to rest too long is to destroy the momentum acquired; to rest too little is to fail in renewing one's strength. Know yourself, and proportion things accordingly. With this reservation, frequent short spells of rest, which refresh without obliging you to make a complete new start afterwards, are the most advantageous.

Ah, if one could work in the heart of nature, one's window open on a fair landscape, so placed that when one was tired one could enjoy a few minutes in the green country; or, if one's thought was at a standstill ask a suggestion from the mountains, from the company of trees and clouds, from the passing animals, instead of painfully enduring one's dull mood—I am sure that the work produced would be doubled, and that it would be far more attractive, far more human.

One is such a realist in the country, and at the same time the soul moves on so high a plane! The categorical imperative was surely not conceived in a meadow, still less the so-called moral arithmetic of a Bentham.

To each young man who aspires to the heights and wants to go far, I say, keep within the reality of human nature. Secure yourself some leisure; do not exhaust yourself; work in tranquillity and in spiritual joy; be free. Use wiles with yourself if necessary; promise yourself in the moment of effort some pleasant relief of which the thought alone will refresh your mind until the moment comes when the actual pleasure will renew your energy.

If you form a group, be considerate about one another's relaxations. St. Thomas says that the man who never jests, who does not take a joke and does not contribute to the amusements or recreations of others is a boor; he is a burden to his neighbor.[1] One cannot live for a single day, said Aristotle, with an utterly gloomy man.

III

This balanced alternation of work and restful joy is all the more necessary because the trials of the worker are many. We have suggested this more than once already. In knowledge, as in everything, one attains salvation only through the cross. Dissatisfaction with oneself, sluggishness of inspiration, the indifference of those about one, envy, misunderstandings, sarcastic remarks, acts of injustice, the desertion of leaders, the falling-away of friends, all these things can be part of the cross, and all of them come in their turn.

"Superiority has to face so many obstacles and to endure so much suffering," wrote George Sand apropos of Balzac, "that the man who fulfils the mission of talent with patience and gentleness is a great man." You will not take the last word to yourself; but if in any degree you become someone, you must expect rare trials and be prepared to taste to the full their different qualities: the trial of the ideal which appears further off the more eagerly you strive to reach it; the trial of fools who do not understand a word of what you say and take scandal at it; the trial of jealous rivals who consider you impudent because you have passed beyond their line of battle; the trial of the good who

[1] 2a 2ae qu. 168, art. 4.

waver in their confidence, suspect you, and throw you over; the trial of the mediocre who form the mass and whom you make uncomfortable by your silent affirmation of a superior world. "If you had been of the world, the world would love its own," declares our Saviour; "but because you are not of the world . . . therefore, the world hateth you." (John 15:19.)

The distractions mentioned above as means of relaxation may help you here also. Everything that affords rest from work helps also to soothe suffering. However, have recourse above all to supernatural means, and among them to work done for a supernatural motive—which is our one and only purpose.

Work cures the pains of work and those of the worker; it is the foe of annoyances, sickness, and sin; it lifts us into a high region where the vexations of life and the weaknesses of the body find alleviation. The urge it rouses, the direction it gives to our energy, are an anodyne for worry and release us from wretched preoccupations.

If you are idle and investigate your body, you will probably feel a good deal of vague discomfort of various kinds; work energetically and you will forget it all. We can say the same about the troubles of the soul. When I ask myself what remedy I shall use against the fits of anxiety and dullness that come over me in my work, I find only one answer: work. What stimulus can I find for my courage, if I lose heart about my work? Work. What means have I of resisting those who are hostile to my endeavor and those others who are jealous of my success? Work. Work is the remedy, work is the balm, work carries me along through every trial. Add to work its companion, silence, and its inspiration, prayer; rest in some loving friendship if God grants it to you, and you can overcome everything.

Work maintains the balance of the soul; it brings about interior unity. Along with the love of God, which regulates the hierarchy of values, it brings our powers into due subordination, and the soul becomes stable. Otherwise, the need for unity can be satisfied only by some hobby or by some passion, and all our weaknesses will resume their sway.

Not in vain is idleness called the mother of all vices; it is also the mother of discouragement and of trials, or at least it contributes to them. The sense of victory springing from work combats such depression; the expenditure of our powers in an orderly rhythm tones them up and regularizes them, giving them something of the spirit of the boat's crew which sings while rowing.

Truth is another defense; it steadies and strengthens us; it gives us delight; in its company we are consoled for our own shortcomings and those of others; its discovery is a reward, its manifestation a noble vengeance on days of contradiction.

The worker is exposed, among other annoyances, to that which is perhaps most keenly felt by the intellectual, and even by the man: criticism does not spare him. When the criticism is superficial and unjust, he is hurt, he is inclined to be irritated; but if it touches his weak point and picks out in his productions or in his character faults that not being able to overcome he would like to forget or conceal, it is then that he is cut to the quick.

What adequate retort can he find and what attitude is he to take up? The same as before. "To every reproach I know now but one answer," says Emerson, "namely to go again to my own work." [1] It is said of St. Thomas also that when he was attacked, which happened much oftener than his posthumous triumph would lead one to suppose, he tried to consolidate his position, to define and clear up his doctrine, and was then silent. "The dumb ox from Sicily" was not going to let himself be turned from his path by the gestures and cries of a crusade of children.

To correct one's mistakes and to keep silence is the great maxim; those who have practiced it have always risen to the heights; they turned the force that aimed at pulling them down into a forward impetus to victory; with the stones cast at them they built their dwelling.

It is childish to defend one's work or to try to establish its worth. Worth defends itself. The solar system does not intervene to settle the dispute between Ptolemy and Copernicus. Truth *is;* true works share in its being and in its power. To fuss and be disturbed about them weakens you. Be silent; humble yourself before God; distrust your

[1] *Journals,* Vol. VIII, p. 171.

judgment, and correct your mistakes; then stay firm as the rock lashed by the waves. The time and strength you would expend in defending a piece of work will be better employed in producing another, and your peace is worth more than some commonplace success.

"The truly wise man does not dispute," writes Keyserling; "he does not defend himself. He speaks or he listens; he states or he tries to discover the meaning of things."

When a reproach is leveled at you, instead of rebelling interiorly or exteriorly like an animal bristling up, observe like a man the bearing of what is said; be impersonal and honest. If the criticism is right and you wrong, do you mean to resist truth? Even if it had its origin in some enmity, have the courage to acknowledge your error, and the noble purpose of utilizing the ill-will that God puts at your service. For evil itself is in the hands of God, and ill-natured criticism, because it is the sharpest, can turn most to your profit.

Having thus drawn your advantage from it, leave the rest to the Lord who judges for you and will do justice in His good time. Do not listen any further. "People do not speak ill," writes St. Augustine, "before the man who does not listen." Envy is a tax levied on the income of glory, distinction, or work. Work, invulnerable in itself, demands its price from the worker. Let him pay and not complain. "Great souls suffer in silence," says Schiller.

When there is nothing to be gotten out of an attack, one must still get oneself out of it—one must come out of it in the first place intact, free from weakening of purpose and from rancor; and then greater, improved by the trial. Real spiritual strength is intensified in persecution; it murmurs sometimes but its murmuring is like that of every creature which "groaneth and travaileth in pain," as the Apostle says.

We have said that intellectual life is heroism: would you want heroism to cost nothing? Things have value in exact proportion to what they cost. Success is for later on; for later on praise, not perhaps that of men but that of God and of His court who will make your conscience their prophet. Your brother workers will also recognize you in spite of their apparent defection. Many little meannesses, and sometimes big villainies, are committed among intellectuals; but a tacit classification none the less puts its seal on real values, even if they are not publicly acknowledged.

If you have to defer your usefulness also until later on—who knows? perhaps until you are no longer in this world—be satisfied; posthumous honor is the most disinterested, and posthumous utility is a sufficient fulfilment of the real purposes of your work. What do you desire? Vain glory? Profit? Then you are but a pseudo-intellectual. Truth? It is eternal. There is no need for eternity to be turned to utility.

Truth is revealed little by little; those who bring it out of the shadow have not the right to ask it to make them a halo; they serve, that is enough; to gird on the hero's sword for a single moment or to carry his shield is their reward.

Is not work worthwhile for its own sake? It is one of the crimes of our age to have belittled it and to have substituted for its beauty the ugliness of fierce self-seeking. Noble souls live a glorious life and expect it to be fruitful in addition. They work not only for the fruit, but for the work; they work in order that their lives may be pure, upright, and manly, like that of Jesus, and ready to be united with His. And so disappointments do not stop them. Love does not fear disappointments, nor does hope, nor faith that has really strong roots.

No matter if one works without apparent fruit, if one sows and does not reap, if one swims and is continually buffeted back from the shore, if one walks and sees nothing ahead but limitless space: none of these things disappoints one who believes and hopes; and they are even a happiness for one who loves, because love is better proved when one works for the pleasure of work, for the pleasure of the beloved and of his service.

IV

However, there are other things in work besides vexations; it has its joys; and it is a happy thing when joy alone disposes us to work and affords us relaxation after our effort.

We ought to be joyous even in afflictions and contradictions, after the example of the Apostle: I exceedingly abound with joy in all our tribulation. Sadness and doubt kill inspiration; but they kill it only when one yields to them. To rise above them by Christian joy is to rekindle the drooping flame.

"The weak brood over the past," writes Marie Bashkirtseff, "the strong take their revenge on it." That can always be done, and to help us to do it, God allows us sometimes to rest in tranquil joy.

A sense of altitude awes but also thrills the soul of the worker; he is like the mountaineer amid rocks and glaciers. The world of ideas opens up scenes more sublime than those of the Alpine landscape, and they fill him with rapture. "To see the order of the universe and the dispositions of divine Providence is an eminently delightful activity," says St. Thomas of Aquin.[1]

According to the Angelic Doctor, contemplation begins in love and ends in joy; it begins in the love of the object and the love of knowledge as an act of life; it ends in the joy of ideal possession and of the ecstasy it causes.[2]

The Catholic intellectual has chosen renunciation; but renunciation enriches him more than proud opulence. He loses the world, and the world is spiritually given to him; he sits on the throne from which the twelve tribes of Israel are judged. (Luke 22:30.) His reality is the ideal; it replaces the other reality and swallows up its blemishes in beauty. Detached from everything in spirit, and very often literally poor, he grows by all that he gives up or that gives him up, for hiddenly he

[1] *In Psalm.* XXVI.

[2] 2a 2ae, qu. 180, art. 1. See pp. ix, 31, 133.

enters again into magnificent possession of it. If he is completely immersed in the most absorbing interior activity, he might from the depth of that apparent sleep say with the Spouse: "I sleep and my heart watcheth." "In my bed by night I sought him whom my soul loveth. . . . I hold him, and I will not let him go."

When one has the necessary dispositions and one's whole soul is in what one is doing, when one studies well, reads well, makes notes well, when one takes unconsciousness and night into one's service, the work that one is preparing is like the seed beneath the sun, or like the child whom its mother brings forth in anguish; but in her joy that a man is born into the world she does not remember the anguish any longer. (John 16:21.)

The reward of a work is to have produced it; the reward of effort is to have grown by it.

It is an astonishing thing that the true intellectual seems to escape those sad effects of age that are death before their time to so many men. He remains young up to the end. One would think that he had a share in the eternal youth of the true. He generally matures early, and is still mature, neither soured nor spoilt, when eternity gathers him in.

This exquisite lasting quality is also found in the saints; it would suggest that sanctity and intellectuality are of the same essence. Indeed, truth is the holiness of the mind; it preserves it; as holiness is the truth of life and tends to fortify it for this world and for the next. There is no virtue without growth, without fruitfulness, without joy; neither is there any intellectual light that does not produce these effects. *Savant* according to its etymology would mean *sage,* and *sagesse,* wisdom, is *one,* comprising the double rule of thought and action.

V

This brings us to the last words we have to say to him who has listened to our theory, short and yet too long, of the intellectual life. "If you follow this course," says St. Thomas to his disciple, "you will bear in the Lord's vineyard foliage and fruit that will be useful all the time of your life. If you put these counsels into practice, you will attain what you desire. Adieu."

Is it not a noble farewell that pledges the honor of truth to him who labors hard and faithfully, assuring whoever fulfils the conditions that he will attain the results he desires? One cannot promise anything to one who has not the necessary gifts. But presupposing the vocation, we have the right to say that cultivation of the mind is not principally the result of genius; it springs from work—properly so-called, organized, and sustained, as we have tried to describe it.

Work creates its instrument for itself. Like the blacksmith who tempers his tools, it forms our character and gives us solidity and therefore confidence.

This confidence which is founded on a natural law is attached to the work rather than to the worker; however the worker also must have faith in himself. Has he not with him the God who said: He that seeketh, findeth, and to him that knocketh, it shall be opened? We all have Truth behind us, and it drives us on through our intelligence; we have it before us, beckoning; above us, inspiring.

The soul is equal in all men; the Spirit breathes in all; what differs, besides degrees of courage, is the brain-structure, with its elements more or less free and active, more or less trammelled; now we know that with our earthly and heavenly helps, we can overcome many deficiencies. The light can trickle in through cracks that our effort widens; when it is there, of itself it extends and intensifies its sway.

We must not lean on ourselves; but to God within us we cannot accord too much trust. We never have too high an idea of the self, if it is the divine self. Besides we may expect a permanent contribution to our resources from those who initiate us into intellectual work, from our friends, and from our fellow-workers. We have the men of genius on our side. Great men are not great for themselves alone; they bear us up; our confidence is implicitly grounded on their existence. With their help, we can make for ourselves a life as great as theirs, except for the disproportion between our powers and theirs. The true intellectual need not fear sterility, inutility: it is enough that a tree be a tree to bear its seed. Results sometimes come late, but they come. The soul gives a return; events give a return. If we cannot rise to the height of what we admire, we can always rise to our own height, and we must say it once again, that is our only goal.

Every individual is unique: therefore every fruit of the spirit is unique also. What is unique is always precious, always necessary. Let us not fail God, and God's success will in part be ours. That can console us for our inferiority, and if we produce anything, encourage us in face of the deluge of books.

Give out all that is in you, and if you are faithful to yourself, and faithful up to the end, you may be sure of attaining the perfection of your work—*your* work, I say, the work that God expects from you and that corresponds to His graces, interior and exterior. At that moment you will have to say to yourself that many works and many lives are finer than yours, but you will be able to add: none is finer for me, and there is no other similar.

I add this also, which is among our motives for confidence: when fidelity is asked of us, and persistent and well-ordered work, this is not meant completely to exclude every lapse; promises made under such a condition would be a mockery. To err is human; but if we hold habitually to what is essential in the prescriptions laid down, that is the sum total about which we are told that it is enough; but that it is indispensable.

It would be desirable that our life should be a flame without smoke or ashes, that no part of it should be lost, that nothing in it should be impure. That cannot be; but what is possible is a fine achievement and its fruits are fair and of rich savor.

Having made up your mind to pay the price, engrave your firm resolution, today if you have not done so already, on the tablets of your heart. I advise you also to write it down in black and white, legibly, and to put the words before your eyes. When you sit down to work, and after praying, you will renew your resolve each day. You will take care to note down especially what is least natural and most necessary for you—for you, as you are. If need be, you will repeat the formula aloud, so that your word may be more explicitly given to yourself.

Then add, and repeat with full certainty: "If you do that, you will bear fruit and you will attain what you desire." Adieu.

Index